William Humphrey

Christian marriage

William Humphrey

Christian marriage

ISBN/EAN: 9783743462885

Manufactured in Europe, USA, Canada, Australia, Japa

Cover: Foto ©ninafisch / pixelio.de

Manufactured and distributed by brebook publishing software (www.brebook.com)

William Humphrey

Christian marriage

BY THE SAME AUTHOR.

THE DIVINE TEACHER. A Letter to a Friend. With a Preface in reply to No. 3 of the English Church Defence Tracts, entitled "Papal Infallibility." Fifth Edition. Cloth, 2s. 6d. Cheap Edition. Wrapper, and without the Preface. 1s.

MARY MAGNIFYING GOD. May Sermons. Fifth Edition. 2s. 6d.

OTHER GOSPELS; or, Lectures on St. Paul's Epistle to the Galatians. Crown 8vo. Cloth. 4s.

THE WRITTEN WORD; or, Considerations on the Sacred Scriptures. 5s.

MR. FITZJAMES STEPHEN AND CARDINAL BELLARMINE. 1s.

THE RELIGIOUS STATE. A Digest of the Doctrine of Suarez contained in his Treatise, "De Statû Religionis," 3 vols. 8vo, 1200 pp., £1 10s.

THE BIBLE AND BELIEF. 2s. 6d.

CHRISTIAN MARRIAGE

BY
THE REV. WILLIAM HUMPHREY, S.J.

LONDON
KEGAN PAUL, TRENCH & CO., 1, PATERNOSTER SQUARE
1886

CHRISTIAN MARRIAGE.

I.

HUMAN society is the work, not of man, but of God. It is constituted, not by the collective will of the human individuals who compose it, but by the single will of God who created them.

God, had He so willed it, might have made mankind to be simply a collection of human individuals, each isolated from the other, and each independent of the other. He might have multiplied men, in the same way as He made man; or He might have ordained some method of production which should have left man as independent of his fellow-man for his human existence, as was the first man Adam.

Had God done so, the formation of human

society might have been still in a certain sense God's work, but not in that sense in which we affirm it to be His work. He might have been the Author of human society in the sense that He is Ruler and Governor of men, but not in that precise and strict sense in which we say that He is the Author of human society as He is the CREATOR of human beings.

God might in that case have been the Founder of human society either mediately or immediately. He might have been its Founder *immediately*, by Himself forming the human beings whom He had created, into a society—co-ordinating the members one with another, and subordinating them to one common head—placing those members under the obligations of law, and investing that head with authority. Or, He might have formed human society *mediately;* and by this we mean,—He might have implanted in men individually a common propension towards coalition into society, in virtue of which the existence of human society would have been the result of the consent and co-operation of the aggregate of human individuals.

He has done this, but He has done more than this. Not only has He implanted in man a natural propension towards society, but He has constituted man, in virtue of His human being, a member of a society. He has made man a member of a human society independently of and antecedently to any act of his own will. It is not that man agrees to be, but, man finds himself, at his entrance into life, a member of a human society, connected by ties with his fellow-men, and subordinated to his fellow-man. He is born into the world not an independent, isolated unit; but a subject, living under law. He has a human superior who has authority over him. His natural superior is that man from whose will and from whose action he has derived his being. The man possesses a natural authority over his own offspring.

In other words and briefly, the family is a society; the family is the foundation of all other human societies; and God is the Author of the family. Man is intended by his Maker to be, man finds himself at his birth to be, and man in virtue of his nature is a member of a family, and so of a human society founded by his Creator.

2.

"It is not good for man to be alone"—was the judgment of the Creator as He beheld His human creature. Man stood surrounded by his fellow-creatures, and man had dominion over them, and yet man stood utterly *alone*. He had no real companion, no friend, for of all those living creatures there was no one that was like unto himself. With all of them he had much in common, but between him and the highest and most perfect of them there stretched a chasm. All that they had he had; but he had also that which they had not. And it was not well, said God, that this should be. *Non est bonum esse hominem solum*—" It is not good that man should be alone."

Without the creation of another human being, man must remain *alone*. The lower animals, his subjects, might increase and multiply, propagate their species, and reproduce themselves; but man, their lord and master, must remain alone in his singleness and his solitude. It might have been good for man, had man been constituted otherwise; but it was not good for man, as God had made him. God might have intended man to be a unit and a solitary, and then in his being solitary and remaining so would have consisted his perfection and wellbeing. But in that case man would have been constituted differently from what he is. From what man is, from what God has made him, we learn the manner of his life, its mode as God intended it to be. God made man to be a member of a society formed of men, sprung from men;—in a word, man is *naturally*, or, in virtue of his nature,—a social being.

3.

There existed in man, as God made him, and therefore there were implanted by God in man certain instincts, inclinations, desires, and cravings which, if man were to remain in his singleness, would never be satisfied. There existed in him also certain faculties which would, in that case, never be exercised, and which would therefore exist in vain. Those instincts, inclinations, desires and cravings were ordained in order to the exercise of these faculties. Both pointed towards an object like to man, but differing from him; and as yet that object did not exist.

There was in man a love for his Maker, there

was in him also a love for his fellow-creatures; and both had their object, and both were satisfied. But there was in him another love, or an, as yet, undeveloped capacity of love, which could only be developed and made actual through the existence of a being like to himself and who should share his own nature.

Hence it was not good that man should be alone, it was not well that there should be only man. It did not become the perfection of the Divine creation. That creation lacked completeness, for it contained a creature, and that creature its crowning glory, with desires unsatisfied and capacities unfulfilled; and so God said,—" Let Us make man a help like unto himself."

4.

There took place another creation of a human soul, there took place another formation of a human body; that human soul was infused into this human body, and the result was that there existed upon the earth another human being. This being was like unto the man, because of the same nature; and yet different from the man, both in body and in soul. This second human body was formed, not from the slime of the earth, but from the substance of the man. Flesh of his flesh, bone of his bone, blood of his blood, there was an essential bond of unity between those two human beings. But along with this unity, there was also an essential diversity: and this very diversity was a second bond of union. Of the same nature as man's own, this body was moulded in a diverse form. It differed in structure and organization.

And as with this second body, so also with that second human soul which was created to tenant it, and to be the principle of its life. There was discernible in those two human souls a unity of similarity, and along therewith a real diversity. Similar in their essence, in their spiritual being, in their powers and faculties, in their capacities for knowledge and judgment and will and choice, they differed as to the mode of their being, and the manner of their processes.

There was, in a word, at once a unity and a difference in the sphere of the psychological as well as in that of the physiological; and both this unity and this difference fitted those two human beings for each other. Man was alone no longer: and God had made for man a help like unto himself.

5.

The Lord God brought to Adam his companion, and Adam called her *Woman*, because she was "taken out of man." God's human creation was now complete. Humanity existed with a diversity of sex in a unity of species and nature. There stood on earth two human *persons*, and they were formed and fitted for each other. It was the design of their common Maker, that they should live in union.

But in the furtherance of this design these two human persons were themselves to co-operate. God would not simply *use* those creatures whom He had made to His own image and likeness. He had made them capable of comprehending His designs, and of associating themselves with Him in carrying out those designs. They were not merely creatures endowed with life only and without understanding, like the animals of His earlier and lower creation. His latest works and His masterpieces resembled Himself in their power of knowledge, and in the freedom of their wills. They were spiritual beings, and they were—persons.

6.

Persons alone are the subjects at once of duty and of right. An irrational creature has no duties towards others, and it has no rights of its own. It may destroy, and it is not morally culpable; it may be destroyed, and it has suffered no injury. Injury is the invasion of right, as culpability is the contradiction of duty. Where there are no rights, there can be no injury; where there is no duty, there can be no moral obligation.

But human persons—as persons—as spiritual beings—moral beings as well as intellectual beings—gifted with power of will no less than with power of understanding—are the subjects of reciprocal duty and of individual right. The failure of this duty is an invasion of that right; and it constitutes—an injury.

7.

When the Lord God brought the first man and the first woman face to face with each other, both were full grown. There was no period of infancy in the dawn of their days. There was in them no gradual evolution of the intellect, no awakening of a dormant will. In the first instant of their being, both knew, understood, judged, willed, and chose. For the determination of their will, and for the acts which flowed from it, each was individually responsible.

Each had a capacity for knowledge, and that capacity in each was satisfied. Each was enlightened with the light of nature; and the law of nature was graven on both their hearts. The pages of the book of nature lay outspread before them; and both could read.

But, besides this, God gave, if not to both,

at least to the man, an infused gift of knowledge. He may have bestowed this also on the woman, or the man may have shared it with her. By his natural knowledge man knew his Maker, and, recognizing his duty as a creature, gave to Him that praise and worship which was His due, and to which he had an essential, an inalienable, and an indefeasible right. By the same knowledge man knew also his own end, and that it was to know, to love, and to serve the Divine Majesty from whom he derived his human being.

By means of his infused knowledge man knew, or at least he knew more fully and in detail, his temporal destiny, and his *natural* end. He knew that he was not to be a solitary in the universe of God—that it was not well that he should stand alone—that he was not intended to exist as an isolated, independent unit—that his destiny in the Divine idea was one of duty towards others like unto, but differing from himself, and that his relation to them was one of right.

The first man and the first woman, as they stood face to face, knew by the evidence of the senses repeated by the testimony of the voice within them—they knew by the light of nature brightened by that further light which God had added—that they were made for each other, and that their natural destiny was—to be one.

8.

Recognizing their destiny as human beings, those two, the first man and the first woman, freely and voluntarily accepted it. An act of real consent, rooted in and springing from a previous act of judgment, was the basis and bond of their union. They entered into a mutual contract, as both were capable of doing ; and the first human contract, the first contract between two human beings, was a contract between a man and a woman, and that contract was—a *matrimonial* contract.

Both man and woman were capable, and equally capable of contracting, for both were *persons;* and as *persons* both were free, and equally free. Both as *persons* had rights as both had duties. Both had personal rights with regard to themselves individually, and each might transfer these personal rights to the other. By such transference the one would become the possession and property of the other; and from such transference new duties would emerge.

A matrimonial contract is effected by mutual matrimonial consent, and its result is the merging of two physically and intellectually individual human persons in one moral personality; or, the formation of one civil person, leading an undivided life, with common interests and goods.

The consent of those two persons in the paradise of pleasure was their own act, but it was an act elicited in obedience to a divine decree, in submission to and union with the divine will. Such consent once given could never be retracted; the contract which it effected could never be rescinded; the bond which it established could never be dissolved. It was the work, as it was the will, of God; and those whom God had joined together, no man might henceforth sunder.

9.

Woman was then, as she is now, the subordinate equal of man; and matrimony made manifest then, as it makes manifest now, the equality of woman with man. Matrimony is at once the manifestation of her equality, and the charter of her rights. Where matrimony is had in honour, the position of woman is secure and her rights are sacred. The matrimonial contract is onerous and bilateral, and it is entered into by freely and mutually consenting equals. The wife belongs to her husband, not by right of conquest or by right of purchase, but by the right of her own self surrender. And as she gives, so she receives. She has given herself; she receives him in return. She belongs to him in property; he is equally her possession. She cannot recall her consent or annul her contract; he is equally powerless. God, and God alone, can sever the matrimonial bond; and the only agent which He employs for its severance is the Angel of Death. The dissolution of the bond which binds together a human body and a human soul in the unity of one human life, must precede the dissolution of that other bond which makes two human beings to be no more twain but one. When the golden link of life is severed, the bond of matrimony is likewise broken. Then—but not till then. While husband and wife both live, their matrimony endures.

10.

Thus was matrimony established in the beginning. And why? Because God had decreed the existence not only of a human being, or of human beings, but of a human *race*. He had constituted His angels in a wonderful order, by their hierarchies and their choirs. But the angels were not a race. No angel reproduced his species. No angel begot, or was begotten. Among them generation and offspring were unknown. It was otherwise with the living creatures of God's lower creation. Among the angels there was a unity of nature with a diversity of order; among the animals there was a unity of nature with a diversity of sex. God arranged them in their several species, and within those species He made them male and female. God so made them that within each species there might be the principle of its preservation and its increase. Thus the species was reproduced, and the individual creatures which composed it multiplied.

In the individuals of the purely animal or brute creation there were implanted by their Maker appetites and instincts. The satisfaction of those appetites was to the animals the motive of their action; and the regulation of that satisfaction was the work of these instincts. In satisfying their innate appetites they attained their end; following their instincts, the divine law regarding them was fulfilled. These instincts were expressions of that law. In following these instincts there was service—but there was no obedience. Obedience requires submission of the will, with knowledge of the law. In the animals there was neither knowledge of law not will to be bound by it. Obedience moreover requires freedom—freedom from extrinsic compulsion and from intrinsic necessity. And the animals are not free. In blindly following their inborn instincts in the satisfaction of their natural appetites, they are intrinsically necessitated by a law of their animal being.

But man is free. Man can have knowledge of the law which ought to regulate his actions, and man may refuse to obey that law. For such refusal every man is individually responsible.

And yet man too has his appetites—appetites of the same nature, and implanted for the same end as that of those which belong to the lower animals of the brute creation; for man is as really an animal as is the lowest of them all.

Man is a microcosm of creation. In man creation finds its centre. Within the circle of his personal unity there coexist the most opposite extremes. Man is spiritual as are the angels; he is animal as are the brute beasts that have no understanding. Man is material as is the earth from which he was taken. There are in man not three souls, but one. But that one soul is at once intellective, sensitive, and vegetative. It is spiritual and it is animal. Apart from the body—disembodied—it can exercise purely spiritual functions; in the body it can also exercise animal functions by means of the organs of the body. Man's material body is the seat of animal appetites. Every one of those animal appetites is in itself good, for every one of them was implanted of set purpose and definite design by the Hand of God. Were any one of those appetites evil, that evil would redound to the God of Nature, and He would be the Author of evil. The pleasure which accompanies the satisfaction of those appetites is also in itself good; and this pleasure was given in order to their exercise and for the promotion of their end. And that end is known to man. Those acts of man's animal appetites which are done in order to their end are so done in accordance with the dictates of man's reason, and in obedience to the higher law of his spiritual nature. They are therefore not only innocent and lawful; they may be also religious and meritorious.

Man's appetites are not ends, but they are means towards an end. That end is known to man's reason, and was ordained by God. Used as means in order to that end man's animal appetites are used reasonably and therefore rightly. When his appetites are satisfied as if they were in themselves ends and means, such satisfaction is irregular, inordinate, and therefore immoral.

II.

God is the God not of anarchy, but of order. When God made man, He established a reign of order within man as well as around him. There was in man, as he was constituted by his Maker, a perfect subordination of the lower to the higher—of the sensitive to the intellective—of the animal to the spiritual—of his body to his soul. The will of man was his highest power; and his will reigned supreme. The exercise of his appetites was subject to the dominion of his will; and the acts of his will were in accordance with the dictates of his reason. This subordination—this reign of order—this supremacy of will in man formed what theologians call *the integrity of his nature.* Man possessed it during the period of his innocence—while his understanding was as yet unclouded, and while as yet his will had never swerved from its obedience to the voice of his conscience and to the law of his Maker. When innocence was lost, integrity was gone. There was in rebel man rebellion of the appetites against the dominion of that will which had itself rebelled. Man had sold himself, in his lust after a freedom which became not the creature, into a captivity and a bondage which was at once his punishment and his dishonour. His corruptible body was from the date of his fall henceforward the arena of a struggle which should endure till that body returned to the dust from which it sprang. Throughout his life he should have to wage a warfare—to subdue his rebellious appetites, and to bring them into subjection to the dominion of his will.

When innocence was gone, and integrity of nature had followed it in its departure, the reign of concupiscence began. Fallen man is the subject of concupiscence; and in his struggle against concupiscence matrimony comes to his aid. Comes to his aid, we say, for this was not the primary end of matrimony; and it is not its principal end now. The primary and the principal end of Matrimony was, and is—*Maternity.*

12.

The Lord God blessed the man and the woman, and said to them—"Increase and multiply, and replenish the earth." When the first woman conceived and brought forth her first born son, she called his name Cain, saying, "I have gotten a man through God." Adam then called his wife's name Eve, when he understood her to be "mother of all the living."

Eve was the mother of mankind; and the motherhood of Eve was a motherhood of sorrow. Had her maternity taken place, like her matrimony, in the state of her innocence, it would have been a maternity of unmingled joy, unaccompanied by suffering, unalloyed by sorrow; but between her matrimony and her maternity her transgression had intervened, and God had said—"I will multiply thy sorrows and thy conceptions, and in sorrow shalt thou bring forth children."

Both parents were penitents, but the period of their innocence was ended; and innocence once gone is gone for ever. Themselves spiritually alive, they were the parents of the spiritually dead. Immaculate conception had been the design of God for every being who was child of man; but this, the design of their Divine Creator, the transgression of the first father of every human being. had frustrated. The offspring of the innocent would have been conceived and born in the state of grace, and of the same unfallen, virgin innocence; but the offspring of the penitent would have to confess with the Psalmist—" I was born in iniquity, and in sin did my mother conceive me."

The first son of man was to slay his own brother; but the mother of the murderer had herself entailed God's curse of death on her murdered child. She had travailed in the wilderness by reason of her sin; and her child while he lived had gazed with her not on the paradise of pleasure whence she had been thrust, but on that earth which the Lord God had cursed. Her husband's life was a life of labour, for God had said to Adam—"Cursed is the earth in thy work; with labour and toil shalt thou eat thereof all the days of thy life; in the sweat of thy face shalt thou eat bread till thou return to the earth out of which thou wast taken, for dust thou art, and into dust thou shall return." Husband and wife alike were clad now no longer in the glory of their innocence, but in garments fashioned from the skins of slain beasts which betokened their degradation.

But, if such was the state of misery to which man had reduced himself, why should he perpetuate this misery in his children? Why, by an act of his own will, give being to others on whom should, through him, be entailed a heritage of sin, of suffering, of sorrow, and of death? Why not end human sin and human suffering and human sorrow with the human lives of those two human beings who had caused them? God willed them to leave behind them on the earth a posterity, it is true, and they knew this. But then, on the other hand, they had already shewn that knowledge of the will of God was not a sufficient motive to cause them to subject their own wills to His. Their fall had not destroyed their freedom; from without there was no compulsion, there was no necessity constraining them from within. Man's will had forfeited its supremacy of dominion over his lower, animal nature, and had henceforth to struggle for the mastery. Among the enemies of his will there was a traitor within the fortress, a foe of man's own household, and that enemy was—the flesh. But God brings good out of evil; and the enemies of God may be pressed into His service, and made to contribute to the accomplishment of His designs. Those very appetites and animal passions which exercise so powerful an influence for evil over fallen man, become the auxiliaries of God.

God wills the preservation of the individual, and the preservation of the species, by the multiplication of the individuals who form it. Towards man's co-operation with God for those two ends, two powerful appetites in man lend efficient aid. Man's appetite for food, and the animal pleasure which accompanies or results from its satisfaction, induces man to do that which is necessary in order to the preservation of his life. Man is led by his appetite to eat, and he is forced to labour in order that he may eat. If there were in man no appetite for food, and no pleasure consequent on its satisfaction, would man as a rule take the means necessary in order to the end—the preservation of his life? Does it consist with our knowledge of human nature, and with our experience of human practice, to suppose that a merely intellectual motive existing in the mind of man, would, in the average man, always so press upon his will as to ensure his spending a considerable portion of his existence in the consumption of the necessary food? Suppose that his eating had been prescribed simply as a duty in order to the refection of his body, and had been a merely mechanical act, like placing the same quantity of food with the same expenditure of pains, and the same loss of time, in an earthen vessel—an act unaccompanied by any pleasureable sensation, and satisfying no inward craving—would man, as a rule, have persevered in taking this trouble? Still more forcibly may we argue, if man had had to labour in the sweat of his brow to earn this food, or, at least, to be put to no small expense, and compelled to deny himself indulgence in pleasures which would have otherwise been within his reach, would he have from day to day persevered in the use of the means necessary to the end of the repair of the daily decay of his corruptible body?

If this be so with regard to an end which most affects the individual man himself—the preservation of his own life—is it not still more certainly and manifestly so with regard to an end which lies outside himself—the preservation of his species?

If the multiplication of his species had been proposed to man simply as a duty, and that in face of all the trouble and expense, and of all the labour and toil and anxiety which the performance of that duty would necessarily entail upon him, would man have undertaken that duty, or persevered in its fulfilment? Would a merely intellectual motive, existing calmly in his mind, have placed and kept sufficient pressure on his will to induce him to create for himself that which would necessitate a drain upon his resources, and, through an increase of expenditure for others, a diminution of the pleasures which he might otherwise have himself enjoyed?

With His perfect knowledge of that which is in man, God has implanted in his human creature the strongest of all passions. He has done this in order to that end which He wills— the continuance of the human race, and the preservation of the human species, by the generation of human individuals. To the means which is necessary for the accomplishment of this divine end, man's will is thus, as it were, instinctively impelled or drawn.

By a natural instinct human beings are led to obey a law of their nature, and they enter voluntarily into that state of matrimony, the end of which is—*maternity*, and the result of maternity is—*offspring*.

13.

But further, not only are the appetites and passions of human beings enlisted in the service of their Maker for the promotion of His designs;

their affections and emotions contribute towards the same end. Chief among these is that of love. Love, moreover, is as diverse as is its object. And love requires an object. Without an object it is not elicited. It exists potentially but it has not actual exercise. There must exist an object in order to that exercise. Such an object exists when a man is joined in matrimony with one on whom his affections have fastened; and when that matrimony is followed by maternity, there exist other beings who are in turn the objects of a diverse love.

By means of matrimony the family is founded; by means of maternity the family idea is completed; and the family is the very theatre of human affection. In the family there is exercised and made manifest in all its wisely and well-ordered diversity that affection of which the human heart is capable. The perfect family is preserved in its unity by the cords of Adam. It is a centre of human affections, of which no two are the same. There is the affection of the husband for his wife; and it differs in its character from the reciprocal affection of the wife for her husband. There is the affection of the father for his son, and it differs from that which the mother equals, if she does not indeed excel him in bestowing. It differs also from that affection with which he regards his daughter; and it again is not the same as that with which the mother loves the child of her own sex. A similar diversity is manifest in the love which the children return to their parents. The son loves his mother as he loves not his father; the daughter loves her father as she loves not her mother; and the love of son and daughter is in neither case the same. No less real and manifest is the diversity of love between brother and sister, and brother and brother, and sister and sister. Well may we say that a perfect human family is the centre of human affections, and that it is the very theatre of human love in its purest form. Here meet the four rivers, with their diverse streams, of conjugal, parental, filial, and fraternal love. These four satisfy, so far as aught created can satisfy, the thirst of love which the Creator has implanted within the heart of His human creature.

Thus, by means of the family does man attain to one of the summits of his natural perfection, and arrive at his truest and purest human happiness.

Outside the family this wealth of human love has no existence. Outside the family man and woman may alike satisfy a lawless passion; outside the family, both parents may love their offspring: but the one love is not—conjugal, and the other is in no true sense—parental.

Outside the pale of matrimony there is no true maternity.

14.

Maternity means more than merely childbearing. Men are not mere animals; and the function of a mother is not ended when she has given her children birth. God does not simply launch His creatures into existence, and leave them to their fate; by His perpetual action He preserves them in existence and supplies their needs. In the production of each human creature, He associates with Himself two human persons; and in their co-operation they must not only obey His laws, but make the method of His action the model of their own. They must care for the sustentation of their children's bodies by the supply of their bodily wants, since otherwise they would sink beneath the level of the brute creation; they must care also and equally for the education of their children's souls. Children are not pet animals; and although they have not yet entered on the full exercise of their rights as persons they are as really human persons as are their parents. They are not merely to be fed and fondled: they are to be reverenced and had in honour as becomes their dignity. As spiritual beings, as gifted with immortal souls, they are, in their personal dignity, the equals of the authors of their material being. Subject to their parents, in virtue of that which from them they have derived, they have duties indeed, but they have rights as well. As spiritual beings they possess intelligences which can be perfected only by a knowledge of the truth; and they possess wills which, in order to their perfection, must be trained towards the good. From ignorance and from evil they have a right to be free; and, so far as it lies within his power, to procure this freedom is the office and duty of a parent.

Philosophers tell us that the good and the true are identified with being, and so consequently with each other. Theologians tell us, that in God these three are essentially one since in Him divine goodness and divine truth are identified with the divine essence; and that from Him all three when found in the creature are derived. As the Author of our being, God is our Father; and, as He is our Father, He is also our Teacher and our Ruler. On our parents lies a shadow of the paternity of Him from Whom all paternity in Heaven and on earth is named; to them therefore it belongs, in virtue of their office, to teach and to rule those personal beings in causing whose existence they have been instrumental. Children then, as *intellectual* and *moral*, or, in a word, as spiritual beings, have a right to look to their parents for that heritage of knowledge and of law which is necessary for the education of their minds and wills. Now, outside the divinely designed and ordered family what guarantee is there for their enjoyment of this their natural right?

As *social* beings, children have a further

right. Man is, as we have seen, a social being; by nature he is formed and fitted, and so marked out as destined to be a member in a society of his fellows. The primary and fundamental human society is that of the family; and man ought to be born into the world of men as a member of a family. True, he may in time himself enter into conjugal relations, and lay the foundations of a family of which he shall be the head; but for many a year he must, if born outside a family, remain, morally at least, if not otherwise, a unit and a solitary amid the surrounding crowd of his fellow-men.

As *moral* beings, moreover, children have yet another right. They have a right to be sustained by the edification of a good example; and this especially they expect to find, and they ought to find in their superiors, and, among their superiors, in their first known, and best known superiors, their immediate superiors who are their parents. Who, moreover, is so much led by example as is a child? He is subject to the influence of example—good or evil—before he is capable of receiving teaching—good or bad. A man is moulded by the intangible moral influences around him; his moral tone varies according to the moral atmosphere he breathes. And if a man, how much more a child? His mother's example is his first lesson. The ideas that first enter his mind are those which have existed in the mind of his mother, which have been clothed in her words, and uttered by her lips. His will has first bent itself beneath the pressure of hers. Hers has been the first authority which he has recognized and obeyed.

What, then, ought not that woman to be who enters on the noble office of a mother, and who has to fulfil the sublime functions of maternity! In order rightly to fulfil these functions she must clearly apprehend, and keep well in view the nobility—the personal dignity of the living and immortal being who has been committed to her charge. As she forgets her child's personal dignity, so will she neglect her own duties, which are the correlatives of its rights. But how shall she remember that dignity, if she has forgotten her own? We have seen that by the contract of matrimony alone is the personal dignity of woman, and her personal equality with man, and her personal freedom recognized, made manifest, and secured. The woman who enters on maternity without having previously lived in matrimony—who is a mother, but not a wife—has renounced her dignity, and forfeited her place of honour. The child of that woman has for mother one from whose head the crown has fallen; and for father the man who has wrought her dishonour.

At his first entrance on the world, that human being is the victim of a wrong.

15.

Man is the lord of creation, for God gave to man dominion. God gave him dominion over the lower creation—over not only inanimate creatures, but over also living, although irrational creatures. Such creatures man may possess, and in them he can establish, retain, exercise, and secure a right of property. To that which is his property—to that of which he acquires lawful possession—to that which, in a word, belongs to him—he has a right; and he who deprives him of this right, inflicts on him an injury and does him wrong.

Man was also master of himself; and this in a twofold sense. Not only was he *dominus sui*, as holding his lower nature and all his subordinate faculties in subjection to the dominion and mastery of his will; but he could also, in a manner, dispose of himself, and cause himself, by his own consent, to become the property of another, so that he should be possessed by and belong to that other, who should in consequence have rights of dominion over him. This man did when the first man entered into the first matrimonial contract.

But previous to this transference of dominion —to this delivery of himself into the power of another—he had himself a right of property in that other. The body of that other human person to whom he now belonged, had been formed from his own substance, and to a right of property in it he had therefore a certain claim.

The first man and the first woman were not in the same position. The man was not formed from the woman, but the woman from the man; and therefore, even after the man was, in virtue of the matrimonial contract, under the dominion of the woman, it still remained true that—" the head of the woman is the man."

By the same right of property, the man has

dominion over his children, inasmuch as they are formed of his substance.

But this right he shares with the woman, inasmuch as they are formed of her substance also.

The common parental right of father and mother over their children rests upon the basis of this fact, that those children are their common offspring.

Here we have, then, in the family, consisting of father and mother and children, a perfect society—one moral whole—a body formed of head and members—constituted and preserved in its moral unity by the existence of one principle and centre of unity, which supposes authority on the one side and subordination on the other.

Such, however, is the perfection of this society, that the exercise of that authority is tempered by duty, and the consequences of that subordination are regulated by right.

These two—duty and right—are divinely united; and in every society which is after the divine idea, must be duly observed.

16.

Among the first duties of a father is that of provision for his children. In order that he should fulfil this duty, he ought to have moral certainty that they are indeed his children. This is reasonable. The motive of his exertion on their behalf is that they are his own—and a reproduction of himself. Hence the necessity of fidelity on the part of the woman. Her fidelity is essential to the matrimonial idea, for without her fidelity the family relations become uncertain, the family rights are weakened in their foundations, and the family duties lose their force of obligation.

Infidelity on the part of the woman, and

consequent uncertainty with regard to the paternity of her children, deprives the man also of another mainspring of exertion. Man covets honours as well as riches; and his honours as well as his riches he accumulates not for himself alone, but for his posterity after him, or, for himself in his posterity. Now, if uncertainty is introduced with regard to his relation to those who, in virtue of the marriage, may legally claim to bear his name, and to reflect his honours as well as to possess his riches, he is deprived of one of the main motives of action which lead men to do good service for the State.

But above all man is by his wife's infidelity defrauded of the full exercise of his paternal love. How can that man love with a father's love one who may be the child of another, and that other his greatest enemy, who has wrought him the most grievous wrong, and done him the foulest dishonour?

Hence we see the real reasonableness of that

social ordinance which visits so heavily a woman's sin against chastity, while similar sins on the man's part are so easily condoned. The man's sin is single, the woman's sin is twofold. Both have sinned against God; in God's sight both are equally guilty, and both merit at God's hands the same punishment. But the woman has sinned *also against society* as the man has not sinned, and cannot sin; and the woman justly meets *at the hands of society* a punishment which is not inflicted on the man. Her conjugal infidelity, by rendering the paternity of her offspring uncertain, has loosened the framework of society. Self-preservation is a law of nature, and it obtains in the case of the aggregate society as it obtains in that of the individual man. Society rightly resents that which is subversive of its interests and, in a manner, of its existence.

As a moral virtue chastity is the same in either sex; but as a *social virtue* it belongs especially to the woman. Chastity is to her what truth and honesty, as social virtues, are to man. That this is the sense of society is apparent from the language of society. We see it in the different sense of the word *honour*, as applied to woman and to man respectively. When we speak of female honour, we mean chastity; the honour of a man is his truth and trustworthiness. These are necessary in him in order to the welfare of society, as chastity and conjugal fidelity are necessary on the woman's part; and a lack of these is visited by society on him as it is not visited by society on her. For a man to be dishonest is *a social crime*, as it is *a social crime* for a woman to be unchaste. As individuals we may extend our charity and restore our friendship to a repentant forger, but society forbids our intrusion of him within its pale. It is not unreasonable that society should treat in like manner a repentant woman who has equally violated its laws. Pharisaism is an evil and a folly: but there is a growth of sentimentalism on this subject in the present day which is, socially, still more mischievous.

17.

We have drawn out the idea of matrimony from the idea of man, as he is a social being; and we have found that in order to the well-being and perfection of society, matrimony must have two essential characteristics—unity and indissolubility. As ordained in the beginning, the matrimonial contract was between one man and one woman; and the contract, once entered into and completed, could not be withdrawn from or dissolved. The unity and the indissolubility of matrimony were therefore of the divine idea and design.

Whatever therefore is opposed to those two essential characteristics—unity and indissolubility—is opposed to the perfection of matrimony as divinely conceived and instituted, and is also subversive of the perfection of human society. Among such evils are polyandry, polygamy, and divorce.

Polyandry is the union of one woman with two or more men—not successively, but simultaneously. This is against the law of nature, and it is condemned by the natural conscience. It shakes the foundations of society, and it is opposed to the primary end of matrimony. The curse of childlessness falls where it prevails, and the fountains of human life are stayed. It is at once a sin against God, and a crime against humanity.

Polygamy is the simultaneous union of one man with more than one woman. This is not opposed to the primary end of matrimony, or to the law of nature. Barrenness does not follow as its result; it tends rather to the multiplication of mankind. It was therefore, not being intrinsically evil, divinely permitted in the infancy of the human race. It is, however opposed to the secondary ends of matrimony, as opposed to the peace and perfection of the family and the family relations, to the undivided mutual love of husband and wife, to the dignity of the woman, and to the welfare of the children. It was divinely prohibited in the primeval institution; and the divine words were—"The man shall cleave to his wife, and they shall be two in one flesh."

Divorce is the dissolution of the matrimonial bond by the annulling of the matrimonial contract; and this also is subversive of the matrimonial idea. The loosening of the bond between husband and wife is a loosening of the bonds which bind together human society.

18.

Human society is the work of God, for it is the result of a principle in human nature, which has God for its author. When men and women wedded and formed families, those families naturally coalesced into tribes; and these tribes again, by an extension of the same natural process, coalesced into peoples. The family had its home; the tribes had their villages, towns, and cities; the people had its commonwealth. The village was the aggregate of homes; the town or city was an extension of the village; the state, kingdom or republic, as the case might be, was the result of a natural coalition of subordinate municipalities under one common ruler. The dominion of the father in his family extended itself with the extension of that family into the kingdom, and its result was the dominion of the king. The royal power is an extension of the paternal power. It is a result, not of social covenant, but of natural evolution. It is a legitimate process of human nature, and, as such, is ordained by the Divine Author of that nature.

Every human society therefore, the most widely extending and the most perfectly developed, as well as the narrowest and the most rudimentary, rests upon the primary society of the family as upon its foundation, and follows it as its type. But matrimony lays the foundation of the family; and so matrimony lies at the root of human society.

19.

Jesus Christ came as the Redeemer of men, and as the Regenerator of society. He entered into relations with mankind collectively, as well as with man individually. He came as the Second Adam, and as the Founder of a new family. In the first Adam the human family fell; in the Second Adam a human family was to rise again. As in Adam men died, so in Christ were men to be made alive. The supernatural life of men was the result of their possession of that habitual, sanctifying grace which is *anima animæ*—the soul of the soul, and which, as such, gives supernatural life to the human soul, as that soul gives natural life to the human body so long as it remains within it. Partakers of this habitual or abiding, sanctifying grace which made them holy, men were made "partakers of the divine nature," and became members of the human family of the sons of God. By Jesus Christ "came grace and truth;" and to as many as believed in Him He gave power to become the sons of God. He came to be a human Father in the supernatural order, and He was to beget sons and daughters unto God.

He founded a Church, which He wedded to Himself, and which He calls His Spouse. He speaks of Himself as the Bridegroom, and of her as His mystic Bride.

She is called His Body, He is called her Head; and the men who compose her are said by His Apostle — and consequently by the Spirit of Truth who inspired him—to be members of His Body, of His Flesh, and of His Bones.

She, in her individual oneness—as a moral person—is indissolubly united to Him. They are "two in one flesh." For her sake he left His Father in Heaven, and His Mother at Nazareth, that He might cleave to that immaculate Spouse who had issued from His opened side as He slept on Calvary.

The end of that matrimony of Jesus with the Church His Bride was her maternity, the existence of a supernatural offspring, and His paternal relation towards those children whom He had begotten again unto God.

The words of Jesus to fallen man were— "You must be born again." As there was a natural process of generation, so there was to be a supernatural process of regeneration. Baptism was the first of those seven sacraments which He ordained as the instruments or vehicles or channels of His grace. By means of baptism men were made recipients of divine grace, were initiated into that new society of which He was the Head—that new family of which He was the Father—and they acquired thereby a right and title to heaven as their inheritance.

As their Father, Jesus made provision for His children alike in sickness and in health. He provided for them, in their spiritual sickness, a means of healing in the sacrament of Penance. For the healed and whole He instituted the sacrament of the Eucharist; He gave Himself —as the Living Bread of Life—for the sustenance and refreshment of their souls. As in life, so in death He cared for them; by the sacrament of Extreme Unction He prepared them for their last agony. That men, moreover, might minister those sacraments to their fellow-men, and to provide for the spiritual education and government of His children, He instituted the sacrament of Order.

So much for the sanctification of individual men; but the Redeemer of men came also for the sanctification of *society*. At the date of His advent human society was sick unto death. It had departed from its primeval type, and in order to its restoration, it must return to its primitive and divine constitution. Polygamy which marred, and divorce which destroyed the very idea of matrimony, obtained in all nations of the earth, and even among the chosen people. Conjugal infidelity and unnatural crimes added to that mass of social cancers which were eating out the very vitals of the body-politic beneath the fairest exteriors of the ancient civilizations. In the Jewish theocracy the foundations of society were shaken as in the commonwealths of Greece and Rome. With the unity and indissolubility of marriage, the dignity of woman had disappeared, and one half of the human race was in a state of degradation. Woman was regarded as a necessary evil, as a piece of property, or as an instrument of pleasure. She was the toy or the slave of man her master. The rottenness of society was the result of her dishonour; the restoration of its soundness rendered necessary the recognition of her human and personal rights.

To restore woman to her rightful place in the economy of the human race, to make man recognize her, acknowledge her, and treat her as his equal—with a personal dignity as perfect as his own—was part of the mission of the Redeemer of mankind. To this end He restored matrimony to its primeval type—as it was "in the beginning of the creation." He resealed it with its two essential characteristics of unity and indissolubility; and prohibited, as subversive of it, polygamy and divorce. He did more. He sanctified it by a sacrament.

Sanctifying matrimony, He sanctified the family; and, sanctifying the family, He sanctified society. Society rested on the family, the family rested on matrimony; and, when the matrimonial contract was elevated to the dignity of a sacrament, society was sanctified in its foundations and at its centre.

The result was Christendom; and, in Christendom, the dignity of woman.

20.

This majestic work of reformation—nay! of almost recreation—was worthy of the divine wisdom and omnipotence. The Catholic Church effected what no civilization and no philosophy had been able to accomplish; and what she did, she alone has retained the power of doing. Human societies for religious purposes outside her pale, are powerless to restrain the violence of human passions backed by the pressure of human power. The Roman Pontiffs have throughout the ages asserted and maintained the rights of woman. In defence of the rights of woman England was lost to the Holy See. Had the Vicar of Him who restored matrimony and invested it with a sacramental dignity sacrificed the rights of one woman to satisfy the lawless desires of her royal husband, he would have sacrificed her sex; and, sacrificing her sex, he would have sacrificed society. Had it been but the sacrifice of a woman, it might have been for the common good; but it was the sacrifice of woman. The Roman Pontiffs speak, not to one age or nation, but to the world and for all time; and never has their divine wisdom and their divine fortitude shone forth more resplendently than when concerning Christian marriage their voice has given no uncertain sound. The Catholic and Roman Church which restored the position of woman, clearly asserts and unflinchingly maintains her rights; and with the Catholic religion her position and her rights are bound up. Within the Catholic Church her dignity is assured; outside that Church she is at the mercy of her master.

The religion which took the place of Catholic Christianity in England has produced its natural and necessary fruit in the legalizing of divorce. A human institution cannot stem the torrent of human passions. A human institution cannot brook superior human force. The laws of England lend their sanction to what the Church of God stigmatizes as adultery; and the idea of Christian marriage is fading from the English mind. They who sow the wind must reap the whirlwind.

There is no mistake as to the issue between the Church and the world. The world in our day is fighting to the death for two things—for secular education and for civil marriage. The

Church claims for herself the decision of all matrimonial causes, and the control of her children in their mental and their moral training. The efforts of the world are hopeless, for the Church of the living God cannot change. Wives and husbands may separate and enter with other men and women into unhallowed unions; but such unions can never be Christian marriages. Legalized adulteries is the mildest term by which Christian men can with truth describe them. Marriage on such terms—and marriage made in contemplation of possible divorce—becomes at best a licensed concubinage.

Well may Christian women love the Roman Pontiffs; they are the sole champions of their Christian dignity, and they have never failed. Well may they mistrust a religion which has been to them but a broken reed—founded in the dishonour of their sex, and established on what its founders sought to make the ruins of Christian matrimony.

PART II.

IN order to complete the true idea in our minds of Christian marriage we must give further consideration to three points :—

1. That Christian matrimony is a true and proper sacrament of the New Law.

2. That there is no real distinction, or possibility of separation between the *contract* of Christian matrimony and the *sacrament* of matrimony: and that consequently, in the case of baptized persons, there is no true matrimony which is not at the same time a sacrament.

3. That the Catholic and Roman Church has power and the right to constitute impediments which shall be antecedently subversive of the

matrimonial contract; and that to her tribunal all causes which concern the bond of matrimony belong—and this not by the concession, either express or tacit, of the civil ruler: but in virtue of her own proper, original and divine right, a right which belongs to her in property in the extreme and exclusive sense that it belongs and can belong to her alone, and that it is inalienable.

I.

That matrimony is truly and properly one of the seven sacraments of the Gospel or New Law—that as such it was instituted by Jesus Christ Himself—and that it confers grace—is a revealed truth of the Catholic faith. This truth was defined by the Catholic Church in the Council of Trent, and its definition was rendered necessary by the heresies which came to a head in the sixteenth century.

Christian matrimony pre-supposes Christian baptism. Baptism is "the gate of the sacraments," and it is the baptized only who are capable of the reception of other sacraments. The matrimony of the unbaptized is therefore not a sacrament. The unbaptized are subjects of the natural law only, and their contracts cannot have any higher sanctions than those which that law affords. The matrimony of the unbaptized is a lawful contract, and a sacred bond, but it does not confer grace, and it is not a sacrament.

It follows that before the Incarnation of the Son of God, and the institution by Him of sacraments as channels of His grace, and among them of the sacrament of baptism, matrimony, however lawful and holy it may have been in itself, and as a *contract*, was not sacramental. As a lawful contract, and in itself, it was sanctified from the beginning by God in Paradise, but it was not a centre and source of sanctification, as is a sacrament, until it was raised to the level and dignity of a sacrament by Jesus Christ.

Like every other sacrament, matrimony confers sanctifying grace. This grace is that the possession of which makes its possessor holy. Hence its name of sanctifying grace. It is also called habitual grace, as distinguished from actual grace. Actual grace is bestowed in order to an act. It is transient as is that act. It passes away. Habitual grace abides. Habitual sanctifying grace once bestowed remains in the soul of its receiver so long as it is not expelled by the commission of mortal sin, the state of which is incompatible in the same soul at the same time with the state of sanctity or holiness. Of this grace baptism bestows the first instalment, and an increase to the amount of it which is already possessed is added by every other sacrament, and consequently by the sacrament of matrimony.

Along with this sanctifying grace, which is habitual and abiding, matrimony confers also a right to actual graces to be bestowed by God in time of need, and in aid of those special needs which matrimonial life entails. This life has of necessity its own sorrows as well as its own joys—its own sufferings as well as its own pleasures—and its own burdens as well as its own solace. The state of matrimony has its duties as well as its rights, and in order to their due fulfilment, the strength of the noblest nature must be supplemented by the strength of divine grace. Apart from all other difficulties, the *unity* of matrimony—or its absolute restriction of a man to one consort—along with its *indissolubility*—or the essentially life-long nature of the bond which nought but death can sunder—would be for the frailty of fallen nature a burden greater than it could bear, were it not for the succours of the grace of God. If human nature, since its fall, were left to itself and to its own resources, novelty of pleasure would by-and-by be swallowed up in satiety, and the love of the senses which seek variety would ere long crave for satisfaction in other objects. The love that is fed by bodily beauty must wither with old age. It is. of its own nature as corruptible and as evanescent as is that from which it springs. It is mortal, and is bound to die, unless grace lends to it a life which is not its own. The love of the senses is blind to its own briefness, and when its eyes are opened its days are ended. It is written in the gospel of the flesh, by one of its apostles, that marriage bonds are needless while love lasts, and that when love has vanished they are intolerable fetters. Amid the mire of this maxim lies sunk a truth which cries for a sacrament from Heaven in aid of man's weakness here on earth. If there is a state of mortal life which requires, nay, demands a sacrament, that state is matrimony. Were we left to the conjecture of our reason, we should expect a sacrament for the benefit of those who bear Christ's yoke as married persons. Taught by God, we know that such a sacrament exists—that it was instituted by the Incarnate Son of God—and that it conveys grace which He merited on that Cross which He reddened with His Precious Blood. This sacramental grace was purchased and is bestowed for the strengthening of the married in their mutual love, in their fidelity to each other, and in their observance of each other's rights—for the well-ordering of their intercourse in accordance not merely with the promptings of sensual love and animal desire, but with the dictates of human reason, and of that reason as enlightened by divine religion—and for the education and government of their children as Christian subjects in a Christian home.

Further, along with this sacramental grace there is bestowed by means of the sacrament of matrimony an increase of theological and of moral virtues, and among these the foremost place is held by the four which claim it—by charity and piety, by fidelity and patience. A married life which is adorned with these jewels is a life which is after the pattern of married life as it exists in the mind of Christ. It is the fruit and flower of a sacrament. It meets the eye as the visible expression of Christian matrimony.

2.

That there is no real distinction or possibility of separation between the *contract* of Christian matrimony and the *sacrament* of matrimony is a Catholic doctrine which is so certain that its contradiction would savour of more than rashness. The sacrament of matrimony is not a rite which supervenes to a contract which is already perfected in itself and apart from that sacrament. It is not a spiritual adornment, or an extrinsic property, or an accidental quality which is superadded to the contract. It is the contract itself, which, remaining physically the same, is by a moral transformation assumed and raised to the nature and dignity, to the level and efficacy of a sacrament. Hence there is not, and there cannot be, any true matrimonial contract between baptized persons which is not of necessity at the same time a sacrament. Whenever in any union of baptized persons there is no sacrament, it is simply and solely because the contract between such persons was invalid, and was therefore not a true matrimonial contract. In every case in which the contract between Christians is matrimonially valid, it is also sacramental. The sacramental nature of the contract does not depend on the faith of the contracting parties—on their belief in sacraments—or on their being aware that matrimony is a sacrament, or that their matrimonial contract is sacramental. The sacramentality of the contract depends solely on two facts—the fact of the validity of the contract—and the fact that it is entered into by persons who had previously been baptized. The sacramentality is entirely independent of their intention, and the only intention which is necessary on their part is that of entering into a valid matrimonial contract.

It follows that the marriages of Protestants—supposing them to have been validly baptized—are as sacramental as are the marriages of Catholics. Their matrimony is as much sacramental as is their baptism. It is as independent of their belief or unbelief, of their knowledge or ignorance of its sacramental nature.

As baptism does not require the ministry of a priest in order to its validity, so neither does matrimony. In matrimony the contracting parties are themselves the ministers of the sacrament, as they are themselves the creators of the contract. It is their matrimonial and mutual consent which effects the matrimonial contract, and it effects through that contract the sacrament which is identified with it. The nuptial benediction of priest or pontiff has no more share in effecting the sacrament than it has in effecting the contract.

Even in those countries in which the disciplinary decree of the Council of Trent against clandestine marriages has been canonically promulgated, and where all marriages are consequently invalid and absolutely null and void, and mere concubinages, which have not been celebrated by the parties in presence of the parish priest or of his duly authorized deputy—the invalidity attaches not merely to the sacrament, but to the contract—and it attaches to the sacrament only through the contract. The sacrament is invalid because the contract is invalid. If the contract were valid, the sacrament would be equally valid. It is not, in the case of those countries, the benediction of the priest which is necessary in order to the validity of the sacrament, but it is the *presence* of the parish priest, which is a necessary condition *sine quâ non* in order to the validity of the contract. He is present not as minister of the sacrament, but as *witness* to the contract—as the *testis approbatus* or approved witness required by the Church in order to the validity of the contract as a matrimonial contract. His benediction is as extrinsic to this contract as it would be to any other contract. His presence as an indispensable witness is as essential to the validity of the matrimonial contract in the cases supposed as the presence of a particular witness would be essential to the validity of any legal contract, for the validity of which the presence of such witness, in addition to the mutual consent of the contracting parties, was required by the law of the land. The benediction of the parish priest does not enter into and it forms no part of the sacrament, and its value is at the most that of a sacramental. The matrimonial contract, and consequently the sacrament of matrimony, if it is celebrated in his presence and in any manner, so as that he is rendered capable of bearing witness to the fact, and however unwilling he might be to witness it or bear testimony to it, is valid. It would be equally valid if he were to withhold his benediction, nay, if he were to lay the contract and all concerned under his curse.

Hence in countries such as England, where the disciplinary decree of Trent has not been promulgated, clandestine marriages of Catholics—or marriages contracted by them without the presence of the priest as witness—are, as well as the marriages of baptized Protestants, valid both sacramentally and as matrimonial contracts; and this whatever may be the nature and measure of the guilt which in the case of recalcitrant Catholics attaches to the contracting parties by reason of their irregular and unlawful action.

It is unlikely that here in England, or in countries where Protestants are in an immense majority, the Trent decree will ever be canonically promulgated, since the effect of requiring the presence of the Catholic parish priest by way of witness, as a condition *sine quâ non* to the validity of all matrimonial contracts within the realm, would be to invalidate the subsequent marriages not only of Catholics who should fail in observance of this condition—a consequence which would not be of such practical inconvenience as to bar legislation, or rather promulgation of existing law—but of all baptized Protestants, and so to deprive their unions of their sacramental dignity and value, and reduce them to the level of civilly legalized concubinages. Such, in the case of baptized persons, non-sacramental unions would undoubtedly be, however little the persons contracting them should, by reason of their ignorance, be morally responsible, or in the absence of all moral guilt.

In this difference of practice or discipline in different countries there is not involved any divergence of doctrine. In every country under heaven the sacrament of matrimony consists in a valid matrimonial contract between baptized persons, but in some countries a condition *sine quâ non* is required in order to the validity of a matrimonial contract, which is not yet required, and which may never, and probably will never be required in other countries. This wise diversity of discipline in accordance with the circumstances of countries, and determined by considerations of the highest charity towards those who, although baptized, have been born into darkness, and live blinded by unbelief, is no more inconsistent with the unity of the Catholic Church than is the diversity of the laws which regulate contracts and determine their validity in England and Scotland and other countries under British rule subversive of the unity of the empire.

As in the case of every other sacrament, the sacrament of matrimony has, besides its ministers, its matter and its form. Since this sacrament consists in the contract, its matter and its form are those of the contract. The remote matter in either case, or rather, under either aspect—since the contract and the sacrament are identified—is the same, namely, the bodies of the contracting parties, or their mutual dominion over each other's bodies for the purposes of married life, which is the object of the contract. The proximate matter and the form are contained in the words or equivalent signs which express the consent which effects the contract. These words are, under different aspects, at once the proximate matter and the form. They are the proximate matter as they express delivery of dominion by one contracting party; they are the form as they signify acceptance by him of the delivery of dominon made in like manner by the other contracting party. There is not merely a mutual delivery of dominion, but there is also a mutual acceptance of such delivery. The delivery on the one part is at the same time the acceptance of the corresponding delivery on the other part. Acceptance following on delivery is the form which completes every contract.

Further, in this, as in every other sacrament, we find a *sign*—a thing signified, and effected as well as signified—and a grace sacramentally conferred. The sign is found in the words which signify the contract. These words effect that which they signify. They effect an indissoluble union, which is henceforth no longer subject to the will and power of the contracting parties. They are powerless to rescind the contract, to dissolve the bond which it has established, or to alienate in favour of others the mutual rights of dominion over each other which it has transferred by way of property. This indissoluble union is a sacramental shadow of the indissoluble union between Christ as Bridegroom and the Church which is His Bride; and that again is a union formed on the pattern of the indissoluble wedding of the two natures—the divine and the human—which subsist in the one Divine Person of the Son of God. In virtue of the words, expressive of matrimonial consent, which complete the matrimonial contract, there is conferred the grace which sanctifies the matrimonial union.

It is clear therefore that nothing is lacking to this matrimonial contract between baptized persons which is required to satisfy the demands of the idea and nature of a Christian sacrament.

3.

That the Catholic and Roman Church has power—and that of inherent and inalienable divine right of which she cannot be deprived, and which she cannot resign—to constitute impediments which shall be antecedently subversive of the matrimonial contract, is of faith and was defined by the Council of Trent.

Her possession of this power follows also from the fact that the matrimonial contract is itself the sacrament of matrimony. It is admitted on all hands as manifest that whatever concerns the sacraments, their administration, and the determination of their validity and lawfulness, belongs to the Church of God and not to the civil ruler. It is equally clear that when a sacrament consists in a contract, with which it is identified and from which it is consequently inseparable, it belongs, and that of necessity and of the nature of the case, to the same church to determine the necessary conditions to the validity as well as to the lawfulness of that contract, and so to determine who are capable, and who are not capable, of contracting. This is, in other words, to determine what are and what are not impediments to the contract; and whether these impediments are merely hindrances to its lawfulness, or are also antecedently subversive of its validity.

Included in this power, which belongs to the Church and to her alone—and which belongs to her of inherent and inalienable because of divine right, and not in virtue of any right bestowed from without, or derived from any civil ruler or earthly power, or of any right which she is free to resign—is the power to abrogate such impediments, or to dispense so that in particular cases they should no longer be impediments. Such dispensations require a cause, but of the adequateness of the cause, or of the lawfulness and advantage of the dispensations, she herself must necessarily be sole judge.

Finally, it also follows that to the tribunal of the Catholic and Roman Church all matrimonial causes belong, and no other tribunal upon the earth has power from God for their decision.

By such matrimonial causes we mean all causes which concern the bond of matrimony, and its validity—all causes of contracts which are antecedent to a matrimonial contract, and which are of themselves and immediately connected with that contract, as are contracts of espousal—all causes which concern consequences of the bond of matrimony, such as the legitimacy of children —and all causes which relate to separation, either temporary or perpetual, of the married persons *a mensâ et thoro*, or either, although without dissolution of the *vinculum*, or bond of matrimony. We do not include among the causes which necessarily belong to the tribunal of the Catholic Church such causes as merely concern money contracts, or civil effects which have been introduced by and depend on civil law, and to which the marriage only gives occasion. These are separable and distinct from the matrimonial contract, and consequently from the sacrament of matrimony. They are therefore, and equally with all purely civil causes, subject to the jurisdiction of the civil ruler.

There are few subjects which more demand attention and the most careful consideration than does that of Christian marriage. In it all men and women have a vested interest, for in one way or in another it concerns every human being. In a special manner does it concern Christians, and all who claim the name of Christian. Men are uneducated as Christians in the Christian religion, if their ideas are vague with regard to a sacrament which is an essential constituent of Christianity. It concerns statesmen also, since the matrimonial contract lies at the foundation of all civil society, and through the sacrament of matrimony all civil society is sanctified. The enemies of the Catholic Church and the enemies of civil society are at one on this matter. The former would wrest the sacrament from the Church's jurisdiction; the latter would rend the contract by robbing it of the indissoluble character which makes it matrimonial. Deprived of its sacramental sanction the contract falls to the level, and will share the fate of other contracts which have become burdensome to those whom they bind. Governments which are merely human, and laws which aim at expressing not the divine law but the will of the masses who create their lawgivers, will be powerless to stay the torrent of human passion, and to set bounds to the licence of human will. Power to do this belongs to one Government alone, and belongs to it because it is, while human in its embodiment, divine in the principle of its life and action, of its thought and will, of its authority and power. The Kingdom of Jesus Christ upon the earth, in which He reigns, and through which He rules— the Catholic and Roman Church—the creator of Christian society, is its one saviour and preserver. By means of the sacrament of matrimony, "Jesus is called to the marriage" of Christian men, and by the power of His will a contract, natural in itself as are the waters which well forth from the earth, is transformed into a sacrament, symbolized by the wine into which at a wedding water was changed by its Creator. The first miracle of Jesus was wrought at a marriage, by means of it He manifested His glory, and by reason of it His disciples believed in Him. The history of Christian matrimony in its indissolubility is the history of a standing miracle—more marvellous in the moral order than was the wonder of Cana in the physical order—a manifestation of the glory of Jesus as He is Ruler of the princes and peoples of the earth throughout the centuries, and a motive of credibility, or ground of our belief in His doctrine, authority, and power.

PRINTED BY WILLIAM CLOWES AND SONS, LIMITED,
LONDON AND BECCLES.

A LIST OF
KEGAN PAUL, TRENCH & CO.'S
PUBLICATIONS.

8. 86

1, *Paternoster Square,*
London.

A LIST OF
KEGAN PAUL, TRENCH & CO.'S
PUBLICATIONS.

CONTENTS.

	PAGE		PAGE
GENERAL LITERATURE.	2	MILITARY WORKS.	35
PARCHMENT LIBRARY.	20	POETRY.	36
PULPIT COMMENTARY.	23	NOVELS AND TALES.	42
INTERNATIONAL SCIENTIFIC SERIES.	32	BOOKS FOR THE YOUNG.	44

GENERAL LITERATURE.

A. K. H. B.—From a Quiet Place. A Volume of Sermons. Crown 8vo, 5s.

ALEXANDER, William, D.D., Bishop of Derry.—The Great Question, and other Sermons. Crown 8vo, 6s.

ALLEN, Rev. R., M.A.—Abraham : his Life, Times, and Travels, 3800 years ago. Second Edition. Post 8vo, 6s.

ALLIES, T. W., M.A.—Per Crucem ad Lucem. The Result of a Life. 2 vols. Demy 8vo, 25s.

A Life's Decision. Crown 8vo, 7s. 6d.

AMHERST, Rev. W. J.—The History of Catholic Emancipation and the Progress of the Catholic Church in the British Isles (chiefly in England) from 1771-1820. 2 vols. Demy 8vo, 24s.

AMOS, Professor Sheldon.—The History and Principles of the Civil Law of Rome. An aid to the Study of Scientific and Comparative Jurisprudence. Demy 8vo. 16s.

Ancient and Modern Britons. A Retrospect. 2 vols. Demy 8vo, 24s.

ANDERDON, Rev. W. H.—Evenings with the Saints. Crown 8vo, 5s.

ANDERSON, David.—"Scenes" in the Commons. Crown 8vo, 5s.

ARISTOTLE.—**The Nicomachean Ethics of Aristotle.** Translated by F. H. Peters, M.A. Second Edition. Crown 8vo, 6*s*.

ARMSTRONG, Richard A., B.A.—**Latter-Day Teachers.** Six Lectures. Small crown 8vo, 2*s*. 6*d*.

AUBERTIN, J. J.—**A Flight to Mexico.** With Seven full-page Illustrations and a Railway Map of Mexico. Crown 8vo, 7*s*. 6*d*.

   Six Months in Cape Colony and Natal. With Illustrations and Map. Crown 8vo, 6*s*.

BADGER, George Percy, D.C.L.—**An English-Arabic Lexicon.** In which the equivalent for English Words and Idiomatic Sentences are rendered into literary and colloquial Arabic. Royal 4to, 80*s*.

BAGEHOT, Walter.—**The English Constitution.** New and Revised Edition. Crown 8vo, 7*s*. 6*d*.

   Lombard Street. A Description of the Money Market. Eighth Edition. Crown 8vo, 7*s*. 6*d*.

   Essays on Parliamentary Reform. Crown 8vo, 5*s*.

   Some Articles on the Depreciation of Silver, and Topics connected with it. Demy 8vo, 5*s*.

BAGOT, Alan, C.E.—**Accidents in Mines:** their Causes and Prevention. Crown 8vo, 6*s*.

   The Principles of Colliery Ventilation. Second Edition, greatly enlarged. Crown 8vo, 5*s*.

   The Principles of Civil Engineering as applied to Agriculture and Estate Management. Crown 8vo, 7*s*. 6*d*.

BAKER, Sir Sherston, Bart.—**The Laws relating to Quarantine.** Crown 8vo, 12*s*. 6*d*.

BAKER, Thomas.—**A Battling Life;** chiefly in the Civil Service. An Autobiography, with Fugitive Papers on Subjects of Public Importance. Crown 8vo, 7*s*. 6*d*.

BALDWIN, Capt. J. H.—**The Large and Small Game of Bengal and the North-Western Provinces of India.** With 20 Illustrations. New and Cheaper Edition. Small 4to, 10*s*. 6*d*.

BALLIN, Ada S. and F. L.—**A Hebrew Grammar.** With Exercises selected from the Bible. Crown 8vo, 7*s*. 6*d*.

BARCLAY, Edgar.—**Mountain Life in Algeria.** With numerous Illustrations by Photogravure. Crown 4to, 16*s*.

BARLOW, James W.—**The Ultimatum of Pessimism.** An Ethical Study. Demy 8vo, 6*s*.

   Short History of the Normans in South Europe. Demy 8vo, 7*s*. 6*d*.

BAUR, *Ferdinand, Dr. Ph.*—A Philological Introduction to Greek and Latin for Students. Translated and adapted from the German, by C. KEGAN PAUL, M.A., and E. D. STONE, M.A. Third Edition. Crown 8vo, 6s.

BAYLY, *Capt. George.*—Sea Life Sixty Years Ago. A Record of Adventures which led up to the Discovery of the Relics of the long-missing Expedition commanded by the Comte de la Perouse. Crown 8vo, 3s. 6d.

BELLASIS, *Edward.*—The Money Jar of Plautus at the Oratory School. An Account of the Recent Representation. With Appendix and 16 Illustrations. Small 4to, sewed, 2s.

The New Terence at Edgbaston. Being Notices of the Performances in 1880 and 1881. With Preface, Notes, and Appendix. Third Issue. Small 4to, 1s. 6d.

BENN, *Alfred W.*—The Greek Philosophers. 2 vols. Demy 8vo, 28s.

Bible Folk-Lore. A Study in Comparative Mythology. Crown 8vo, 10s. 6d.

BIRD, *Charles, F.G.S.*—Higher Education in Germany and England. Being a brief Practical Account of the Organization and Curriculum of the German Higher Schools. With critical Remarks and Suggestions with reference to those of England. Small crown 8vo, 2s. 6d.

BLECKLY, *Henry.*—Socrates and the Athenians: An Apology. Crown 8vo, 2s. 6d.

BLOOMFIELD, *The Lady.*—Reminiscences of Court and Diplomatic Life. New and Cheaper Edition. With Frontispiece. Crown 8vo, 6s.

BLUNT, *The Ven. Archdeacon.*—The Divine Patriot, and other Sermons. Preached in Scarborough and in Cannes. New and Cheaper Edition. Crown 8vo, 4s. 6d.

BLUNT, *Wilfrid S.*—The Future of Islam. Crown 8vo, 6s.

Ideas about India. Crown 8vo. Cloth, 6s.

BODDY, *Alexander A.*—To Kairwân the Holy. Scenes in Muhammedan Africa. With Route Map, and Eight Illustrations by A. F. JACASSEY. Crown 8vo, 6s.

BOSANQUET, *Bernard.*—Knowledge and Reality. A Criticism of Mr. F. H. Bradley's "Principles of Logic." Crown 8vo, 9s.

BOUVERIE-PUSEY, *S. E. B.*—Permanence and Evolution. An Inquiry into the Supposed Mutability of Animal Types. Crown 8vo, 5s.

BOWEN, *H. C., M.A.*—Studies in English. For the use of Modern Schools. Eighth Thousand. Small crown 8vo, 1s. 6d.

English Grammar for Beginners. Fcap. 8vo, 1s.

Simple English Poems. English Literature for Junior Classes. In four parts. Parts I., II., and III., 6d. each. Part IV., 1s. Complete, 3s.

BRADLEY, F. H.—**The Principles of Logic.** Demy 8vo, 16s.

BRIDGETT, Rev. T. E.—History of the Holy Eucharist in Great Britain. 2 vols. Demy 8vo, 18s.

BROOKE, Rev. S. A.—Life and Letters of the Late Rev. F. W. Robertson, M.A. Edited by.
    I. Uniform with Robertson's Sermons. 2 vols. With Steel Portrait. 7s. 6d.
    II. Library Edition. With Portrait. 8vo, 12s.
    III. A Popular Edition. In 1 vol., 8vo, 6s.

    The Fight of Faith. Sermons preached on various occasions. Fifth Edition. Crown 8vo, 7s. 6d.

    The Spirit of the Christian Life. Third Edition. Crown 8vo, 5s.

    Theology in the English Poets.—Cowper, Coleridge, Wordsworth, and Burns. Fifth Edition. Post 8vo, 5s.

    Christ in Modern Life. Sixteenth Edition. Crown 8vo, 5s.

    Sermons. First Series. Thirteenth Edition. Crown 8vo, 5s.

    Sermons. Second Series. Sixth Edition. Crown 8vo, 5s.

BROWN, Rev. J. Baldwin, B.A.—The Higher Life. Its Reality, Experience, and Destiny. Sixth Edition. Crown 8vo, 5s.

    Doctrine of Annihilation in the Light of the Gospel of Love. Five Discourses. Fourth Edition. Crown 8vo, 2s. 6d.

    The Christian Policy of Life. A Book for Young Men of Business. Third Edition. Crown 8vo, 3s. 6d.

BROWN, Horatio F.—Life on the Lagoons. With two Illustrations and Map. Crown 8vo, 6s.

BROWNE, H. L.—Reason and Religious Belief. Crown 8vo, 3s. 6d.

BURDETT, Henry C.—Help in Sickness—Where to Go and What to Do. Crown 8vo, 1s. 6d.

    Helps to Health. The Habitation—The Nursery—The Schoolroom and—The Person. With a Chapter on Pleasure and Health Resorts. Crown 8vo, 1s. 6d.

BURKE, The Late Very Rev. T. N.—His Life. By W. J. FITZPATRICK. 2 vols. With Portrait. Demy 8vo, 30s.

BURTON, Mrs. Richard.—The Inner Life of Syria, Palestine, and the Holy Land. Post 8vo, 6s.

CAPES, J. M.—The Church of the Apostles: an Historical Inquiry. Demy 8vo, 9s.

Carlyle and the Open Secret of His Life. By HENRY LARKIN. Demy 8vo, 14s.

CARPENTER, W. B., LL.D., M.D., F.R.S., etc.—**The Principles of Mental Physiology.** With their Applications to the Training and Discipline of the Mind, and the Study of its Morbid Conditions. Illustrated. Sixth Edition. 8vo, 12s.

Catholic Dictionary. Containing some Account of the Doctrine, Discipline, Rites, Ceremonies, Councils, and Religious Orders of the Catholic Church. By WILLIAM E. ADDIS and THOMAS ARNOLD, M.A. Third Edition. Demy 8vo, 21s.

CHEYNE, Rev. T. K.—**The Prophecies of Isaiah.** Translated with Critical Notes and Dissertations. 2 vols. Third Edition. Demy 8vo, 25s.

Circulating Capital. Being an Inquiry into the Fundamental Laws of Money. An Essay by an East India Merchant. Small crown 8vo, 6s.

CLAIRAUT.—**Elements of Geometry.** Translated by Dr. KAINES. With 145 Figures. Crown 8vo, 4s. 6d.

CLAPPERTON, Jane Hume.—**Scientific Meliorism and the Evolution of Happiness.** Large crown 8vo, 8s. 6d.

CLARKE, Rev. Henry James, A.K.C.—**The Fundamental Science.** Demy 8vo, 10s. 6d.

CLAYDEN, P. W.—**Samuel Sharpe.** Egyptologist and Translator of the Bible. Crown 8vo, 6s.

CLIFFORD, Samuel.—**What Think Ye of the Christ?** Crown 8vo, 6s.

CLODD, Edward, F.R.A.S.—**The Childhood of the World:** a Simple Account of Man in Early Times. Seventh Edition. Crown 8vo, 3s.
 A Special Edition for Schools. 1s.

 The Childhood of Religions. Including a Simple Account of the Birth and Growth of Myths and Legends. Eighth Thousand. Crown 8vo, 5s.
 A Special Edition for Schools. 1s. 6d.

 Jesus of Nazareth. With a brief sketch of Jewish History to the Time of His Birth. Small crown 8vo, 6s.

COGHLAN, J. Cole, D.D.—**The Modern Pharisee and other Sermons.** Edited by the Very Rev. H. H. DICKINSON, D.D., Dean of Chapel Royal, Dublin. New and Cheaper Edition. Crown 8vo, 7s. 6d.

COLE, George R. Fitz-Roy.—**The Peruvians at Home.** Crown 8vo, 6s.

COLERIDGE, Sara.—**Memoir and Letters of Sara Coleridge.** Edited by her Daughter. With Index. Cheap Edition. With Portrait. 7s. 6d.

Collects Exemplified. Being Illustrations from the Old and New Testaments of the Collects for the Sundays after Trinity. By the Author of " A Commentary on the Epistles and Gospels." Edited by the Rev. JOSEPH JACKSON. Crown 8vo, 5*s.*

CONNELL, *A. K.*—**Discontent and Danger in India.** Small crown 8vo, 3*s.* 6*d.*

The Economic Revolution of India. Crown 8vo, 4*s.* 6*d.*

COOK, *Keningale, LL.D.*—**The Fathers of Jesus.** A Study of the Lineage of the Christian Doctrine and Traditions. 2 vols. Demy 8vo, 28*s.*

CORY, *William.*—**A Guide to Modern English History.** Part I.—MDCCCXV.-MDCCCXXX. Demy 8vo, 9*s.* Part II.—MDCCCXXX.-MDCCCXXXV., 15*s.*

COTTERILL, *H. B.*—**An Introduction to the Study of Poetry.** Crown 8vo, 7*s.* 6*d.*

COTTON, *H. J. S.*—**New India, or India in Transition.** Third Edition. Crown 8vo, 4*s.* 6*d.*

COUTTS, *Francis Burdett Money.*—**The Training of the Instinct of Love.** With a Preface by the Rev. EDWARD THRING, M.A. Small crown 8vo, 2*s.* 6*d.*

COX, *Rev. Sir George W., M.A., Bart.*—**The Mythology of the Aryan Nations.** New Edition. Demy 8vo, 16*s.*

Tales of Ancient Greece. New Edition. Small crown 8vo, 6*s.*

A Manual of Mythology in the form of Question and Answer. New Edition. Fcap. 8vo, 3*s.*

An Introduction to the Science of Comparative Mythology and Folk-Lore. Second Edition. Crown 8vo. 7*s.* 6*d.*

COX, *Rev. Sir G. W., M.A., Bart., and JONES, Eustace Hinton.*—**Popular Romances of the Middle Ages.** Third Edition, in 1 vol. Crown 8vo, 6*s.*

COX, *Rev. Samuel, D.D.*—**A Commentary on the Book of Job.** With a Translation. Second Edition. Demy 8vo. 15*s.*

Salvator Mundi; or, Is Christ the Saviour of all Men? Tenth Edition. Crown 8vo, 5*s.*

The Larger Hope. A Sequel to "Salvator Mundi." Second Edition. 16mo, 1*s.*

The Genesis of Evil, and other Sermons, mainly expository. Third Edition. Crown 8vo, 6*s.*

Balaam. An Exposition and a Study. Crown 8vo, 5*s.*

Miracles. An Argument and a Challenge. Crown 8vo, 2*s.* 6*d.*

CRAVEN, *Mrs.*—**A Year's Meditations.** Crown 8vo, 6*s.*

CRAWFURD, Oswald.—**Portugal, Old and New.** With Illustrations and Maps. New and Cheaper Edition. Crown 8vo, 6s.

CROZIER, John Beattie, M.B.—**The Religion of the Future.** Crown 8vo, 6s.

CUNNINGHAM, W., B.D.—**Politics and Economics:** An Essay on the Nature of the Principles of Political Economy, together with a survey of Recent Legislation. Crown 8vo, 5s.

DANIELL, Clarmont.—**The Gold Treasure of India.** An Inquiry into its Amount, the Cause of its Accumulation, and the Proper Means of using it as Money. Crown 8vo, 5s.

Discarded Silver: a Plan for its Use as Money. Small crown, 8vo, 2s.

DANIEL, Gerard. **Mary Stuart: a Sketch and a Defence.** Crown 8vo, 5s.

DAVIDSON, Rev. Samuel, D.D., LL.D.—**Canon of the Bible:** Its Formation, History, and Fluctuations. Third and Revised Edition. Small crown 8vo, 5s.

The Doctrine of Last Things contained in the New Testament compared with the Notions of the Jews and the Statements of Church Creeds. Small crown 8vo, 3s. 6d.

DAWSON, Geo., M.A. **Prayers, with a Discourse on Prayer.** Edited by his Wife. First Series. Ninth Edition. Crown 8vo, 3s. 6d.

Prayers, with a Discourse on Prayer. Edited by GEORGE ST. CLAIR. Second Series. Crown 8vo, 6s.

Sermons on Disputed Points and Special Occasions. Edited by his Wife. Fourth Edition. Crown 8vo, 6s.

Sermons on Daily Life and Duty. Edited by his Wife. Fourth Edition. Crown 8vo, 6s.

The Authentic Gospel, and other Sermons. Edited by GEORGE ST. CLAIR, F.G.S. Third Edition. Crown 8vo, 6s.

Biographical Lectures. Edited by GEORGE ST. CLAIR, F.G.S. Large crown, 8vo, 7s. 6d.

DE JONCOURT, Madame Marie.—**Wholesome Cookery.** Third Edition. Crown 8vo, 3s. 6d.

Democracy in the Old World and the New. By the Author of "The Suez Canal, the Eastern Question, and Abyssinia," etc. Small crown 8vo, 2s. 6d.

DENT, H. C.—**A Year in Brazil.** With Notes on Religion, Meteorology, Natural History, etc. Maps and Illustrations. Demy 8vo, 18s.

Discourse on the Shedding of Blood, and The Laws of War. Demy 8vo, 2s. 6d.

DOUGLAS, Rev. Herman.—Into the Deep ; or, The Wonders of the Lord's Person. Crown 8vo, 2s. 6d.

DOWDEN, Edward, LL.D.—Shakspere : a Critical Study of his Mind and Art. Eighth Edition. Post 8vo, 12s.

Studies in Literature, 1789-1877. Third Edition. Large post 8vo, 6s.

Dulce Domum. Fcap. 8vo, 5s.

DU MONCEL, Count.—The Telephone, the Microphone, and the Phonograph. With 74 Illustrations. Third Edition. Small crown 8vo, 5s.

DURUY, Victor.—History of Rome and the Roman People. Edited by Prof. MAHAFFY. With nearly 3000 Illustrations. 4to. 6 vols. in 12 parts, 30s. each vol.

EDGEWORTH, F. Y.—Mathematical Psychics. An Essay on the Application of Mathematics to Social Science. Demy 8vo, 7s. 6d.

Educational Code of the Prussian Nation, in its Present Form. In accordance with the Decisions of the Common Provincial Law, and with those of Recent Legislation. Crown 8vo, 2s. 6d.

Education Library. Edited by PHILIP MAGNUS :—

An Introduction to the History of Educational Theories. By OSCAR BROWNING, M.A. Second Edition. 3s. 6d.

Old Greek Education. By the Rev. Prof. MAHAFFY, M.A. Second Edition. 3s. 6d.

School Management. Including a general view of the work of Education, Organization and Discipline. By JOSEPH LANDON. Fifth Edition. 6s.

EDWARDES, Major-General Sir Herbert B.—Memorials of his Life and Letters. By his Wife. With Portrait and Illustrations. 2 vols. Demy 8vo. 36s.

ELSDALE, Henry.—Studies in Tennyson's Idylls. Crown 8vo, 5s.

Emerson's (Ralph Waldo) Life. By OLIVER WENDELL HOLMES. English Copyright Edition. With Portrait. Crown 8vo, 6s.

Enoch the Prophet. The Book of. Archbishop LAURENCE'S Translation, with an Introduction by the Author of "The Evolution of Christianity." Crown 8vo, 5s.

Eranus. A Collection of Exercises in the Alcaic and Sapphic Metres. Edited by F. W. CORNISH, Assistant Master at Eton. Second Edition. Crown 8vo, 2s.

EVANS, Mark.—The Story of Our Father's Love, told to Children. Sixth and Cheaper Edition. With Four Illustrations. Fcap. 8vo, 1s. 6d.

"Fan Kwae" at Canton before Treaty Days 1825-1844. By an old Resident. With Frontispiece. Crown 8vo, 5*s.*

Faith of the Unlearned, The. Authority, apart from the Sanction of Reason, an Insufficient Basis for It. By "One Unlearned." Crown 8vo, 6*s.*

FEIS, Jacob.—**Shakspere and Montaigne.** An Endeavour to Explain the Tendency of Hamlet from Allusions in Contemporary Works. Crown 8vo, 5*s.*

FLOREDICE, W. H.—**A Month among the Mere Irish.** Small crown 8vo. Second Edition. 3*s.* 6*d.*

Frank Leward. Edited by CHARLES BAMPTON. Crown 8vo, 7*s.* 6*d.*

FULLER, Rev. Morris.—**The Lord's Day; or, Christian Sunday.** Its Unity, History, Philosophy, and Perpetual Obligation. Sermons. Demy 8vo, 10*s.* 6*d.*

GARDINER, Samuel R., and J. BASS MULLINGER, M.A.—**Introduction to the Study of English History.** Second Edition. Large crown 8vo, 9*s.*

GARDNER, Dorsey.—**Quatre Bras, Ligny, and Waterloo.** A Narrative of the Campaign in Belgium, 1815. With Maps and Plans. Demy 8vo, 16*s.*

GELDART, E. M.—**Echoes of Truth.** Sermons, with a Short Selection of Prayers and an Introductory Sketch, by the Rev. C. B. UPTON. Crown 8vo, 6*s.*

Genesis in Advance of Present Science. A Critical Investigation of Chapters I.-IX. By a Septuagenarian Beneficed Presbyter. Demy 8vo. 10*s.* 6*d.*

GEORGE, Henry.—**Progress and Poverty:** An Inquiry into the Causes of Industrial Depressions, and of Increase of Want with Increase of Wealth. The Remedy. Fifth Library Edition. Post 8vo, 7*s.* 6*d.* Cabinet Edition. Crown 8vo, 2*s.* 6*d.* Also a Cheap Edition. Limp cloth, 1*s.* 6*d.* Paper covers, 1*s.*

Protection, or Free Trade. An Examination of the Tariff Question, with especial regard to the Interests of Labour. Crown 8vo, 5*s.*

Social Problems. Fourth Thousand. Crown 8vo, 5*s.* Cheap Edition. Paper covers, 1*s.*

GLANVILL, Joseph.—**Scepsis Scientifica;** or, Confest Ignorance, the Way to Science; in an Essay of the Vanity of Dogmatizing and Confident Opinion. Edited, with Introductory Essay, by JOHN OWEN. Elzevir 8vo, printed on hand-made paper, 6*s.*

Glossary of Terms and Phrases. Edited by the Rev. H. PERCY SMITH and others. Second and Cheaper Edition. Medium 8vo, 7*s.* 6*d.*

GLOVER, F., M.A.—**Exempla Latina.** A First Construing Book, with Short Notes, Lexicon, and an Introduction to the Analysis of Sentences. Second Edition. Fcap. 8vo, 2s.

GOLDSMID, Sir Francis Henry, Bart., Q.C., M.P.—**Memoir of.** With Portrait. Second Edition, Revised. Crown 8vo, 6s.

GOODENOUGH, Commodore J. G.—**Memoir of,** with Extracts from his Letters and Journals. Edited by his Widow. With Steel Engraved Portrait. Third Edition. Crown 8vo, 5s.

GORDON, Major-Genl. C. G.—**His Journals at Kartoum.** Printed from the original MS. With Introduction and Notes by A. EGMONT HAKE. Portrait, 2 Maps, and 30 Illustrations. Two vols., demy 8vo, 21s. Also a Cheap Edition in 1 vol., 6s.

Gordon's (General) Last Journal. A Facsimile of the last Journal received in England from GENERAL GORDON. Reproduced by Photo-lithography. Imperial 4to, £3 3s.

Events in his Life. From the Day of his Birth to the Day of his Death, By Sir H. W. GORDON. With Maps and Illustrations. Demy 8vo, 18s.

GOSSE, Edmund.—Seventeenth Century Studies. A Contribution to the History of English Poetry. Demy 8vo, 10s. 6d.

GOULD, Rev. S. Baring, M.A.—**Germany, Present and Past.** New and Cheaper Edition. Large crown 8vo, 7s. 6d.

GOWAN, Major Walter E.—**A. Ivanoff's Russian Grammar.** (16th Edition.) Translated, enlarged, and arranged for use of Students of the Russian Language. Demy 8vo, 6s.

GOWER, Lord Ronald. **My Reminiscences.** MINIATURE EDITION, printed on hand-made paper, limp parchment antique, 10s. 6d.

Last Days of Mary Antoinette. An Historical Sketch. With Portrait and Facsimiles. Fcap. 4to, 10s. 6d.

Notes of a Tour from Brindisi to Yokohama, 1883-1884. Fcap. 8vo, 2s. 6d.

GRAHAM, William, M.A.—**The Creed of Science,** Religious, Moral, and Social. Second Edition, Revised. Crown 8vo, 6s.

The Social Problem, in its Economic, Moral, and Political Aspects. Demy 8vo, 14s.

GREY, Rowland.—**In Sunny Switzerland.** A Tale of Six Weeks. Second Edition. Small crown 8vo, 5s.

Lindenblumen and other Stories. Small crown 8vo, 5s.

GRIMLEY, Rev. H. N., M.A.—**Tremadoc Sermons, chiefly on the Spiritual Body, the Unseen World, and the Divine Humanity.** Fourth Edition. Crown 8vo, 6s.

GUSTAFSON, Alex.—**The Foundation of Death.** Third Edition. Crown 8vo, 5s.

GUSTAFSON, Alex.—continued.

Some Thoughts on Moderation. Reprinted from a Paper read at the Reeve Mission Room, Manchester Square, June 8, 1885. Crown 8vo, 1s.

HADDON, Caroline.—**The Larger Life, Studies in Hinton's Ethics.** Crown 8vo, 5s.

HAECKEL, Prof. Ernst.—**The History of Creation.** Translation revised by Professor E. RAY LANKESTER, M.A., F.R.S. With Coloured Plates and Genealogical Trees of the various groups of both Plants and Animals. 2 vols. Third Edition. Post 8vo, 32s.

The History of the Evolution of Man. With numerous Illustrations. 2 vols. Post 8vo, 32s.

A Visit to Ceylon. Post 8vo, 7s. 6d.

Freedom in Science and Teaching. With a Prefatory Note by T. H. HUXLEY, F.R.S. Crown 8vo, 5s.

HALF-CROWN SERIES :—

A Lost Love. By ANNA C. OGLE [Ashford Owen].

Sister Dora : a Biography. By MARGARET LONSDALE.

True Words for Brave Men : a Book for Soldiers and Sailors. By the late CHARLES KINGSLEY.

Notes of Travel : being Extracts from the Journals of Count VON MOLTKE.

English Sonnets. Collected and Arranged by J. DENNIS.

Home Songs for Quiet Hours. By the Rev. Canon R. H. BAYNES.

Hamilton, Memoirs of Arthur, B.A., of Trinity College, Cambridge. Crown 8vo, 6s.

HARRIS, William.—**The History of the Radical Party in Parliament.** Demy 8vo, 15s.

HARROP, Robert.—**Bolingbroke.** A Political Study and Criticism. Demy 8vo, 14s.

HART, Rev. J. W. T.—**The Autobiography of Judas Iscariot.** A Character Study. Crown 8vo, 3s. 6d.

HAWEIS, Rev. H. R., M.A.—**Current Coin.** Materialism—The Devil—Crime—Drunkenness—Pauperism—Emotion—Recreation —The Sabbath. Fifth Edition. Crown 8vo, 5s.

Arrows in the Air. Fifth Edition. Crown 8vo, 5s.

Speech in Season. Fifth Edition. Crown 8vo, 5s.

Thoughts for the Times. Thirteenth Edition. Crown 8vo, 5s.

Unsectarian Family Prayers. New Edition. Fcap. 8vo, 1s. 6d.

HAWKINS, Edwards Comerford.—Spirit and Form. Sermons preached in the Parish Church of Leatherhead. Crown 8vo, 6s.

HAWTHORNE, Nathaniel.—Works. Complete in Twelve Volumes. Large post 8vo, 7s. 6d. each volume.

> VOL. I. TWICE-TOLD TALES.
> II. MOSSES FROM AN OLD MANSE.
> III. THE HOUSE OF THE SEVEN GABLES, AND THE SNOW IMAGE.
> IV. THE WONDERBOOK, TANGLEWOOD TALES, AND GRANDFATHER'S CHAIR.
> V. THE SCARLET LETTER, AND THE BLITHEDALE ROMANCE.
> VI. THE MARBLE FAUN. [Transformation.]
> VII. } OUR OLD HOME, AND ENGLISH NOTE-BOOKS.
> VIII. }
> IX. AMERICAN NOTE-BOOKS.
> X. FRENCH AND ITALIAN NOTE-BOOKS.
> XI. SEPTIMIUS FELTON, THE DOLLIVER ROMANCE, FANSHAWE, AND, IN AN APPENDIX, THE ANCESTRAL FOOTSTEP.
> XII. TALES AND ESSAYS, AND OTHER PAPERS, WITH A BIOGRAPHICAL SKETCH OF HAWTHORNE.

HEATH, Francis George.—Autumnal Leaves. Third and cheaper Edition. Large crown 8vo, 6s.

> Sylvan Winter. With 70 Illustrations. Large crown 8vo, 14s.

HENNESSY, Sir John Pope.—Ralegh in Ireland. With his Letters on Irish Affairs and some Contemporary Documents. Large crown 8vo, printed on hand-made paper, parchment, 10s. 6d.

HENRY, Philip.—Diaries and Letters of. Edited by MATTHEW HENRY LEE, M.A. Large crown 8vo, 7s. 6d.

HINTON, J.—Life and Letters. With an Introduction by Sir W. W. GULL, Bart., and Portrait engraved on Steel by C. H. Jeens. Fifth Edition. Crown 8vo, 8s. 6d.

> Philosophy and Religion. Selections from the Manuscripts of the late James Hinton. Edited by CAROLINE HADDON. Second Edition. Crown 8vo, 5s.

> The Law Breaker, and The Coming of the Law. Edited by MARGARET HINTON. Crown 8vo, 6s.

> The Mystery of Pain. New Edition. Fcap. 8vo, 1s.

Hodson of Hodson's Horse; or, Twelve Years of a Soldier's Life in India. Being extracts from the Letters of the late Major W. S. R. Hodson. With a Vindication from the Attack of Mr. Bosworth Smith. Edited by his brother, G. H. HODSON, M.A. Fourth Edition. Large crown 8vo, 5s.

HOLTHAM, E. G.—Eight Years in Japan, 1873-1881. Work, Travel, and Recreation. With three Maps. Large crown 8vo, 9s.

Homology of Economic Justice. An Essay by an East India Merchant. Small crown 8vo, 5s.

HOOPER, Mary.—Little Dinners: How to Serve them with Elegance and Economy. Twentieth Edition. Crown 8vo, 2s. 6d.

Cookery for Invalids, Persons of Delicate Digestion, and Children. Fifth Edition. Crown 8vo, 2s. 6d.

Every-Day Meals. Being Economical and Wholesome Recipes for Breakfast, Luncheon, and Supper. Sixth Edition. Crown 8vo, 2s. 6d.

HOPKINS, Ellice.—Work amongst Working Men. Sixth Edition. Crown 8vo, 3s. 6d.

HORNADAY, W. T.—Two Years in a Jungle. With Illustrations. Demy 8vo, 21s.

HOSPITALIER, E.—The Modern Applications of Electricity. Translated and Enlarged by JULIUS MAIER, Ph.D. 2 vols. Second Edition, Revised, with many additions and numerous Illustrations. Demy 8vo, 12s. 6d. each volume.

VOL. I.—Electric Generators, Electric Light.
VOL. II.—Telephone : Various Applications ; Electrical Transmission of Energy.

HOWARD, Robert, M.A.—The Church of England and other Religious Communions. A course of Lectures delivered in the Parish Church of Clapham. Crown 8vo, 7s. 6d.

HUMPHREY, Rev. William.—The Bible and Belief. A Letter to a Friend. Small Crown 8vo, 2s. 6d.

HUNTER, William C.—Bits of Old China. Small crown 8vo, 6s.

HUNTINGFORD, Rev. E., D.C.L.—The Apocalypse. With a Commentary and Introductory Essay. Demy 8vo, 5s.

HUTCHINSON, H.—Thought Symbolism, and Grammatic Illusions. Being a Treatise on the Nature, Purpose, and Material of Speech. Crown 8vo, 2s. 6d.

HUTTON, Rev. C. F.—Unconscious Testimony ; or, The Silent Witness of the Hebrew to the Truth of the Historical Scriptures. Crown 8vo, 2s. 6d.

HYNDMAN, H. M.—The Historical Basis of Socialism in England. Large crown 8vo, 8s. 6d.

IDDESLEIGH, Earl of.—The Pleasures, Dangers, and Uses of Desultory Reading. Fcap. 8vo, in Whatman paper cover, 1s.

IM THURN, Everard F.—Among the Indians of Guiana. Being Sketches, chiefly anthropologic, from the Interior of British Guiana. With 53 Illustrations and a Map. Demy 8vo, 18s.

JACCOUD, Prof. S.—**The Curability and Treatment of Pulmonary Phthisis.** Translated and edited by MONTAGU LUBBOCK, M.D. Demy 8vo, 15s.

Jaunt in a Junk : A Ten Days' Cruise in Indian Seas. Large crown 8vo, 7s. 6d.

JENKINS, E., and RAYMOND, J.—**The Architect's Legal Handbook.** Third Edition, revised. Crown 8vo, 6s.

JENKINS, Rev. Canon R. C.—**Heraldry : English and Foreign.** With a Dictionary of Heraldic Terms and 156 Illustrations. Small crown 8vo, 3s. 6d.

JERVIS, Rev. W. Henley.—**The Gallican Church and the Revolution.** A Sequel to the History of the Church of France, from the Concordat of Bologna to the Revolution. Demy 8vo, 18s.

JOEL, L.—**A Consul's Manual and Shipowner's and Shipmaster's Practical Guide in their Transactions Abroad.** With Definitions of Nautical, Mercantile, and Legal Terms; a Glossary of Mercantile Terms in English, French, German, Italian, and Spanish ; Tables of the Money, Weights, and Measures of the Principal Commercial Nations and their Equivalents in British Standards; and Forms of Consular and Notarial Acts. Demy 8vo, 12s.

JOHNSTON, H. H., F.Z.S.—**The Kilima-njaro Expedition.** A Record of Scientific Exploration in Eastern Equatorial Africa, and a General Description of the Natural History, Languages, and Commerce of the Kilima-njaro District. With 6 Maps, and over 80 Illustrations by the Author. Demy 8vo, 21s.

JOYCE, P. W., LL.D., etc.—**Old Celtic Romances.** Translated from the Gaelic. Crown 8vo, 7s. 6d.

KAUFMANN, Rev. M., B.A.—**Socialism : its Nature, its Dangers, and its Remedies considered.** Crown 8vo, 7s. 6d.

Utopias ; or, Schemes of Social Improvement, from Sir Thomas More to Karl Marx. Crown 8vo, 5s.

KAY, David, F.R.G.S.—**Education and Educators.** Crown 8vo, 7s. 6d.

KAY, Joseph.—**Free Trade in Land.** Edited by his Widow. With Preface by the Right Hon. JOHN BRIGHT, M.P. Seventh Edition. Crown 8vo, 5s.

*** Also a cheaper edition, without the Appendix, but with a Revise of Recent Changes in the Land Laws of England, by the RIGHT HON. G. OSBORNE MORGAN, Q.C., M.P. Cloth, 1s. 6d. Paper covers, 1s.

KELKE, W. H. H.—**An Epitome of English Grammar for the Use of Students.** Adapted to the London Matriculation Course and Similar Examinations. Crown 8vo, 4s. 6d.

KEMPIS, Thomas à.—**Of the Imitation of Christ.** Parchment Library Edition.—Parchment or cloth, 6*s.*; vellum, 7*s.* 6*d.* The Red Line Edition, fcap. 8vo, red edges, 2*s.* 6*d.* The Cabinet Edition, small 8vo, cloth limp, 1*s.*; cloth boards, red edges, 1*s.* 6*d.* The Miniature Edition, red edges, 32mo, 1*s.*

_{*} All the above Editions may be had in various extra bindings.

KETTLEWELL, Rev. S.—**Thomas à Kempis and the Brothers of Common Life.** With Portrait. Crown 8vo, 7*s.* 6*d.*

KIDD, Joseph, M.D.—**The Laws of Therapeutics;** or, the Science and Art of Medicine. Second Edition. Crown 8vo, 6*s.*

KINGSFORD, Anna, M.D.—**The Perfect Way in Diet.** A Treatise advocating a Return to the Natural and Ancient Food of our Race. Second Edition. Small crown 8vo, 2*s.*

KINGSLEY, Charles, M.A.—**Letters and Memories of his Life.** Edited by his Wife. With two Steel Engraved Portraits, and Vignettes on Wood. Fifteenth Cabinet Edition. 2 vols. Crown 8vo, 12*s.*

_{*} Also a People's Edition, in one volume. With Portrait. Crown 8vo, 6*s.*

All Saints' Day, and other Sermons. Edited by the Rev. W. HARRISON. Third Edition. Crown 8vo, 7*s.* 6*d.*

True Words for Brave Men. A Book for Soldiers' and Sailors' Libraries. Eleventh Edition. Crown 8vo, 2*s.* 6*d.*

KNOX, Alexander A.—**The New Playground;** or, Wanderings in Algeria. New and Cheaper Edition. Large crown 8vo, 6*s.*

Land Concentration and Irresponsibility of Political Power, as causing the Anomaly of a Widespread State of Want by the Side of the Vast Supplies of Nature. Crown 8vo, 5*s.*

LANDON, Joseph.—**School Management;** Including a General View of the Work of Education, Organization, and Discipline. Fifth Edition. Crown 8vo, 6*s.*

LEE, Rev. F. G., D.C.L.—**The Other World;** or, Glimpses of the Supernatural. 2 vols. A New Edition. Crown 8vo, 15*s.*

Letters from an Unknown Friend. By the Author of "Charles Lowder." With a Preface by the Rev. W. H. CLEAVER. Fcap. 8vo, 1*s.*

Leward, Frank. Edited by CHARLES BAMPTON. Crown 8vo, 7*s.* 6*d.*

LEWIS, Edward Dillon.—**A Draft Code of Criminal Law and Procedure.** Demy 8vo, 21*s.*

Life of a Prig. By ONE. Third Edition. Fcap. 8vo, 3*s.* 6*d.*

LILLIE, Arthur, M.R.A.S.—**The Popular Life of Buddha.** Containing an Answer to the Hibbert Lectures of 1881. With Illustrations. Crown 8vo, 6*s.*

Kegan Paul, Trench & Co.'s Publications. 17

LLOYD, *Walter.*—The Hope of the World : An Essay on Universal Redemption. Crown 8vo, 5*s.*

LONGFELLOW, H. *Wadsworth.*—Life. By his Brother, SAMUEL LONGFELLOW. With Portraits and Illustrations. 2 vols. Demy 8vo, 28*s.*

LONSDALE, *Margaret.*—Sister Dora : a Biography. With Portrait. Cheap Edition. Small crown 8vo, 2*s.* 6*d.*

George Eliot: Thoughts upon her Life, her Books, and Herself. Second Edition. Small crown 8vo, 1*s.* 6*d.*

LOUNSBURY, *Thomas R.*—James Fenimore Cooper. With Portrait. Crown 8vo, 5*s.*

LOWDER, *Charles.*—A Biography. By the Author of "St. Teresa." New and Cheaper Edition. Crown 8vo. With Portrait. 3*s.* 6*d.*

LÜCKES, *Eva C. E.*—Lectures on General Nursing, delivered to the Probationers of the London Hospital Training School for Nurses. Crown 8vo, 2*s.* 6*d.*

LYALL, *William Rowe, D.D.*—Propædeia Prophetica ; or, The Use and Design of the Old Testament Examined. New Edition. With Notices by GEORGE C. PEARSON, M.A., Hon. Canon of Canterbury. Demy 8vo, 10*s.* 6*d.*

LYTTON, *Edward Bulwer, Lord.*—Life, Letters and Literary Remains. By his Son, the EARL OF LYTTON. With Portraits, Illustrations and Facsimiles. Demy 8vo. Vols. I. and II., 32*s.*

MACAULAY, *G. C.*—Francis Beaumont : A Critical Study. Crown 8vo, 5*s.*

MAC CALLUM, *M. W.*—Studies in Low German and High German Literature. Crown 8vo, 6*s.*

MACHIAVELLI, *Niccolò.* — Life and Times. By Prof. VILLARI. Translated by LINDA VILLARI. 4 vols. Large post 8vo, 48*s.*

MACHIAVELLI, *Niccolò.*—Discourses on the First Decade of Titus Livius. Translated from the Italian by NINIAN HILL THOMSON, M.A. Large crown 8vo, 12*s.*

The Prince. Translated from the Italian by N. H. T. Small crown 8vo, printed on hand-made paper, bevelled boards, 6*s.*

MACKENZIE, *Alexander.*—How India is Governed. Being an Account of England's Work in India. Small crown 8vo, 2*s.*

MAGNUS, *Mrs.*—About the Jews since Bible Times. From the Babylonian Exile till the English Exodus. Small crown 8vo, 6*s.*

MAGUIRE, *Thomas.* —Lectures on Philosophy. Demy 8vo, 9*s.*

MAIR, *R. S., M.D., F.R.C.S.E.*—The Medical Guide for Anglo-Indians. Being a Compendium of Advice to Europeans in India, relating to the Preservation and Regulation of Health. With a Supplement on the Management of Children in India. Second Edition. Crown 8vo, limp cloth, 3*s.* 6*d.*

C

MALDEN, *Henry Elliot.*—Vienna, 1683. The History and Consequences of the Defeat of the Turks before Vienna, September 12th, 1683, by John Sobieski, King of Poland, and Charles Leopold, Duke of Lorraine. Crown 8vo, 4s. 6d.

Many Voices. A volume of Extracts from the Religious Writers of Christendom from the First to the Sixteenth Century. With Biographical Sketches. Crown 8vo, cloth extra, red edges, 6s.

MARKHAM, *Capt. Albert Hastings, R.N.*—The Great Frozen Sea : A Personal Narrative of the Voyage of the *Alert* during the Arctic Expedition of 1875-6. With 6 Full-page Illustrations, 2 Maps, and 27 Woodcuts. Sixth and Cheaper Edition. Crown 8vo, 6s.

MARTINEAU, *Gertrude.*—Outline Lessons on Morals. Small crown 8vo, 3s. 6d.

MAUDSLEY, *H., M.D.*—Body and Will. Being an Essay concerning Will, in its Metaphysical, Physiological, and Pathological Aspects. 8vo, 12s.

Natural Causes and Supernatural Seemings. Crown 8vo, 6s.

McGRATH, *Terence.*—Pictures from Ireland. New and Cheaper Edition. Crown 8vo, 2s.

MEREDITH, *M.A.*—Theotokos, the Example for Woman. Dedicated, by permission, to Lady Agnes Wood. Revised by the Venerable Archdeacon DENISON. 32mo, limp cloth, 1s. 6d.

MILLER, *Edward.*—The History and Doctrines of Irvingism ; or, The so-called Catholic and Apostolic Church. 2 vols. Large post 8vo, 25s.

The Church in Relation to the State. Large crown 8vo, 7s. 6d.

MITCHELL, *Lucy M.*—A History of Ancient Sculpture. With numerous Illustrations, including 6 Plates in Phototype. Super royal 8vo, 42s.

MITFORD, *Bertram.*—Through the Zulu Country. Its Battlefields and its People. With Five Illustrations. Demy 8vo, 14s.

MOCKLER, *E.*—A Grammar of the Baloochee Language, as it is spoken in Makran (Ancient Gedrosia), in the Persia-Arabic and Roman characters. Fcap. 8vo, 5s.

MOLESWORTH, *Rev. W. Nassau, M.A.*—History of the Church of England from 1660. Large crown 8vo, 7s. 6d.

MORELL, *J. R.*—Euclid Simplified in Method and Language. Being a Manual of Geometry. Compiled from the most important French Works, approved by the University of Paris and the Minister of Public Instruction. Fcap. 8vo, 2s. 6d.

MORGAN, *C. Lloyd.*—The Springs of Conduct. An Essay in Evolution. Large crown 8vo, cloth, 7s. 6d.

MORRIS, George.—**The Duality of all Divine Truth in our Lord Jesus Christ.** For God's Self-manifestation in the Impartation of the Divine Nature to Man. Large crown 8vo, 7s. 6d.

MORSE, E. S., Ph.D.—**First Book of Zoology.** With numerous Illustrations. New and Cheaper Edition. Crown 8vo, 2s. 6d.

NELSON, J. H., M.A.—**A Prospectus of the Scientific Study of the Hindû Law.** Demy 8vo, 9s.

NEWMAN, Cardinal.—**Characteristics from the Writings of.** Being Selections from his various Works. Arranged with the Author's personal Approval. Seventh Edition. With Portrait. Crown 8vo, 6s.

** A Portrait of Cardinal Newman, mounted for framing, can be had, 2s. 6d.

NEWMAN, Francis William.—**Essays on Diet.** Small crown 8vo, cloth limp, 2s.

New Truth and the Old Faith: Are they Incompatible? By a Scientific Layman. Demy 8vo, 10s. 6d.

New Social Teachings. By POLITICUS. Small crown 8vo, 5s.

NICOLS, Arthur, F.G.S., F.R.G.S.—**Chapters from the Physical History of the Earth:** an Introduction to Geology and Palæontology. With numerous Illustrations. Crown 8vo, 5s.

NOEL, The Hon. Roden.—**Essays on Poetry and Poets.** Demy 8vo, 12s.

NOPS, Marianne.—**Class Lessons on Euclid.** Part I. containing the First Two Books of the Elements. Crown 8vo, 2s. 6d.

Nuces: EXERCISES ON THE SYNTAX OF THE PUBLIC SCHOOL LATIN PRIMER. New Edition in Three Parts. Crown 8vo, each 1s.

** The Three Parts can also be had bound together, 3s.

OATES, Frank, F.R.G.S.—**Matabele Land and the Victoria Falls.** A Naturalist's Wanderings in the Interior of South Africa. Edited by C. G. OATES, B.A. With numerous Illustrations and 4 Maps. Demy 8vo, 21s.

O'CONNOR, T. P., M.P.—**The Parnell Movement.** With a Sketch of Irish Parties from 1843. Large crown 8vo, 7s. 6d.

OGLE, W., M.D., F.R.C.P.—**Aristotle on the Parts of Animals.** Translated, with Introduction and Notes. Royal 8vo, 12s. 6d.

O'HAGAN, Lord, K.P.—**Occasional Papers and Addresses.** Large crown 8vo, 7s. 6d.

O'MEARA, Kathleen.—**Frederic Ozanam**, Professor of the Sorbonne: His Life and Work. Second Edition. Crown 8vo, 7s. 6d.

Henri Perreyve and his Counsels to the Sick. Small crown 8vo, 5s.

One and a Half in Norway. A Chronicle of Small Beer. By Either and Both. Small crown 8vo, 3s. 6d.

O'NEIL, *the late Rev. Lord.*—Sermons. With Memoir and Portrait. Crown 8vo, 6s.

    Essays and Addresses. Crown 8vo, 5s.

Only Passport to Heaven, The. By One who has it. Small crown 8vo, 1s. 6d.

OSBORNE, *Rev. W. A.*—The Revised Version of the New Testament. A Critical Commentary, with Notes upon the Text. Crown 8vo, 5s.

OTTLEY, *H. Bickersteth.*—The Great Dilemma. Christ His Own Witness or His Own Accuser. Six Lectures. Second Edition. Crown 8vo, 3s. 6d.

Our Public Schools—Eton, Harrow, Winchester, Rugby, Westminster, Marlborough, The Charterhouse. Crown 8vo, 6s.

OWEN, *F. M.*—John Keats: a Study. Crown 8vo, 6s.

    Across the Hills. Small crown 8vo, 1s. 6d.

OWEN, *Rev. Robert, B.D.*—Sanctorale Catholicum; or, Book of Saints. With Notes, Critical, Exegetical, and Historical. Demy 8vo, 18s.

OXONIENSIS.—Romanism, Protestantism, Anglicanism. Being a Layman's View of some questions of the Day. Together with Remarks on Dr. Littledale's "Plain Reasons against joining the Church of Rome." Crown 8vo, 3s. 6d.

PALMER, *the late William.*—Notes of a Visit to Russia in 1840-1841. Selected and arranged by JOHN H. CARDINAL NEWMAN, with Portrait. Crown 8vo, 8s. 6d.

    Early Christian Symbolism. A Series of Compositions from Fresco Paintings, Glasses, and Sculptured Sarcophagi. Edited by the Rev. Provost NORTHCOTE, D.D., and the Rev. Canon BROWNLOW, M.A. With Coloured Plates, folio, 42s., or with Plain Plates, folio, 25s.

Parchment Library. Choicely Printed on hand-made paper, limp parchment antique or cloth, 6s.; vellum, 7s. 6d. each volume.

    The Poetical Works of John Milton. 2 vols.

    Letters and Journals of Jonathan Swift. Selected and edited, with a Commentary and Notes, by STANLEY LANE POOLE.

    De Quincey's Confessions of an English Opium Eater. Reprinted from the First Edition. Edited by RICHARD GARNETT.

    The Gospel according to Matthew, Mark, and Luke.

Parchment Library—*continued*.

Selections from the Prose Writings of Jonathan Swift. With a Preface and Notes by STANLEY LANE-POOLE and Portrait.

English Sacred Lyrics.

Sir Joshua Reynolds's Discourses. Edited by EDMUND GOSSE.

Selections from Milton's Prose Writings. Edited by ERNEST MYERS.

The Book of Psalms. Translated by the Rev. T. K. CHEYNE, M.A.

The Vicar of Wakefield. With Preface and Notes by AUSTIN DOBSON.

English Comic Dramatists. Edited by OSWALD CRAWFURD.

English Lyrics.

The Sonnets of John Milton. Edited by MARK PATTISON. With Portrait after Vertue.

French Lyrics. Selected and Annotated by GEORGE SAINTSBURY. With a Miniature Frontispiece designed and etched by H. G. Glindoni.

Fables by Mr. John Gay. With Memoir by AUSTIN DOBSON, and an Etched Portrait from an unfinished Oil Sketch by Sir Godfrey Kneller.

Select Letters of Percy Bysshe Shelley. Edited, with an Introduction, by RICHARD GARNETT.

The Christian Year. Thoughts in Verse for the Sundays and Holy Days throughout the Year. With Miniature Portrait of the Rev. J. Keble, after a Drawing by G. Richmond, R.A.

Shakspere's Works. Complete in Twelve Volumes.

Eighteenth Century Essays. Selected and Edited by AUSTIN DOBSON. With a Miniature Frontispiece by R. Caldecott.

Q. Horati Flacci Opera. Edited by F. A. CORNISH, Assistant Master at Eton. With a Frontispiece after a design by L. Alma Tadema, etched by Leopold Lowenstam.

Edgar Allan Poe's Poems. With an Essay on his Poetry by ANDREW LANG, and a Frontispiece by Linley Sambourne.

Shakspere's Sonnets. Edited by EDWARD DOWDEN. With a Frontispiece etched by Leopold Lowenstam, after the Death Mask.

English Odes. Selected by EDMUND GOSSE. With Frontispiece on India paper by Hamo Thornycroft, A.R.A.

Parchment Library—*continued.*

Of the Imitation of Christ. By THOMAS à KEMPIS. A revised Translation. With Frontispiece on India paper, from a Design by W. B. Richmond.

Poems: Selected from PERCY BYSSHE SHELLEY. Dedicated to Lady Shelley. With a Preface by. RICHARD GARNETT and a Miniature Frontispiece.

PARSLOE, Joseph.—**Our Railways.** Sketches, Historical and Descriptive. With Practical Information as to Fares and Rates, etc., and a Chapter on Railway Reform. Crown 8vo, 6s.

PASCAL, Blaise.—**The Thoughts of.** Translated from the Text of Auguste Molinier, by C. KEGAN PAUL. Large crown 8vo, with Frontispiece, printed on hand-made paper, parchment antique, or cloth, 12s.; vellum, 15s.

PAUL, Alexander.—**Short Parliaments.** A History of the National Demand for frequent General Elections. Small crown 8vo, 3s. 6d.

PAUL, C. Kegan.—**Biographical Sketches.** Printed on hand-made paper, bound in buckram. Second Edition. Crown 8vo, 7s. 6d.

PEARSON, Rev. S.—**Week-day Living.** A Book for Young Men and Women. Second Edition. Crown 8vo, 5s.

PENRICE, Major J.—**Arabic and English Dictionary of the Koran.** 4to, 21s.

PESCHEL, Dr. Oscar.—**The Races of Man and their Geographical Distribution.** Second Edition. Large crown 8vo, 9s.

PHIPSON, E.—**The Animal Lore of Shakspeare's Time.** Including Quadrupeds, Birds, Reptiles, Fish and Insects. Large post 8vo, 9s.

PIDGEON, D.—**An Engineer's Holiday**; or, Notes of a Round Trip from Long. 0° to 0°. New and Cheaper Edition. Large crown 8vo, 7s. 6d.

Old World Questions and New World Answers. Second Edition. Large crown 8vo, 7s. 6d.

Plain Thoughts for Men. Eight Lectures delivered at Forester's Hall, Clerkenwell, during the London Mission, 1884. Crown 8vo, cloth, 1s. 6d; paper covers, 1s.

POE, Edgar Allan.—**Works of.** With an Introduction and a Memoir by RICHARD HENRY STODDARD. In 6 vols. With Frontispieces and Vignettes. Large crown 8vo, 6s. each.

POPE, J. Buckingham. — **Railway Rates and Radical Rule.** Trade Questions as Election Tests. Crown 8vo, 2s. 6d.

PRICE, Prof. Bonamy. — **Chapters on Practical Political Economy.** Being the Substance of Lectures delivered before the University of Oxford. New and Cheaper Edition. Crown 8vo, 5s.

Kegan Paul, Trench & Co.'s Publications. 23

Pulpit Commentary, The. (Old Testament Series.) Edited by the Rev. J. S. EXELL, M.A., and the Rev. Canon H. D. M. SPENCE.

Genesis. By the Rev. T. WHITELAW, M.A. With Homilies by the Very Rev. J. F. MONTGOMERY, D.D., Rev. Prof. R. A. REDFORD, M.A., LL.B., Rev. F. HASTINGS, Rev. W. ROBERTS, M.A. An Introduction to the Study of the Old Testament by the Venerable Archdeacon FARRAR, D.D., F.R.S.; and Introductions to the Pentateuch by the Right Rev. H. COTTERILL, D.D., and Rev. T. WHITELAW, M.A. Eighth Edition. 1 vol., 15s.

Exodus. By the Rev. Canon RAWLINSON. With Homilies by Rev. J. ORR, Rev. D. YOUNG, B.A., Rev. C. A. GOODHART, Rev. J. URQUHART, and the Rev. H. T. ROBJOHNS. Fourth Edition. 2 vols., 18s.

Leviticus. By the Rev. Prebendary MEYRICK, M.A. With Introductions by the Rev. R. COLLINS, Rev. Professor A. CAVE, and Homilies by Rev. Prof. REDFORD, LL.B., Rev. J. A. MACDONALD, Rev. W. CLARKSON, B.A., Rev. S. R. ALDRIDGE, LL.B., and Rev. McCHEYNE EDGAR. Fourth Edition. 15s.

Numbers. By the Rev. R. WINTERBOTHAM, LL.B. With Homilies by the Rev. Professor W. BINNIE, D.D., Rev. E. S. PROUT, M.A., Rev. D. YOUNG, Rev. J. WAITE, and an Introduction by the Rev. THOMAS WHITELAW, M.A. Fourth Edition. 15s.

Deuteronomy. By the Rev. W. L. ALEXANDER, D.D. With Homilies by Rev. C. CLEMANCE, D.D., Rev. J. ORR, B.D., Rev. R. M. EDGAR, M.A., Rev. D. DAVIES, M.A. Fourth edition. 15s.

Joshua. By Rev. J. J. LIAS, M.A. With Homilies by Rev. S. R. ALDRIDGE, LL.B., Rev. R. GLOVER, REV. E. DE PRESSENSÉ, D.D., Rev. J. WAITE, B.A., Rev. W. F. ADENEY, M.A.; and an Introduction by the Rev. A. PLUMMER, M.A. Fifth Edition. 12s. 6d.

Judges and Ruth. By the Bishop of Bath and Wells, and Rev. J. MORISON, D.D. With Homilies by Rev. A. F. MUIR, M.A., Rev. W. F. ADENEY, M.A., Rev. W. M. STATHAM, and Rev. Professor J. THOMSON, M.A. Fifth Edition. 10s. 6d.

1 Samuel. By the Very Rev. R. P. SMITH, D.D. With Homilies by Rev. DONALD FRASER, D.D., Rev. Prof. CHAPMAN, and Rev. B. DALE. Sixth Edition. 15s.

1 Kings. By the Rev. JOSEPH HAMMOND, LL.B. With Homilies by the Rev. E. DE PRESSENSÉ, D.D., Rev. J. WAITE, B.A., Rev. A. ROWLAND, LL.B., Rev. J. A. MACDONALD, and Rev. J. URQUHART. Fourth Edition. 15s.

Pulpit Commentary, The—*continued.*

1 Chronicles. By the Rev. Prof. P. C. BARKER, M.A., LL.B. With Homilies by Rev. Prof. J. R. THOMSON, M.A., Rev. R. TUCK, B.A., Rev. W. CLARKSON, B.A., Rev. F. WHITFIELD, M.A., and Rev. RICHARD GLOVER. 15*s.*

Ezra, Nehemiah, and Esther. By Rev. Canon G. RAWLINSON, M.A. With Homilies by Rev. Prof. J. R. THOMSON, M.A., Rev. Prof. R. A. REDFORD, LL.B., M.A., Rev. W. S. LEWIS, M.A., Rev. J. A. MACDONALD, Rev. A. MACKENNAL, B.A., Rev. W. CLARKSON, B.A., Rev. F. HASTINGS, Rev. W. DINWIDDIE, LL.B., Rev. Prof. ROWLANDS, B.A., Rev. G. WOOD, B.A., Rev. Prof. P. C. BARKER, M.A., LL.B., and the Rev. J. S. EXELL, M.A. Sixth Edition. 1 vol., 12*s.* 6*d.*

Jeremiah. (Vol. I.) By the Rev. T. K. CHEYNE, M.A. With Homilies by the Rev. W. F. ADENEY, M.A., Rev. A. F. MUIR, M.A., Rev. S. CONWAY, B.A., Rev. J. WAITE, B.A., and Rev. D. YOUNG, B.A. Second Edition. 15*s.*

Jeremiah (Vol. II.) and Lamentations. By Rev. T. K. CHEYNE, M.A. With Homilies by Rev. Prof. J. R. THOMSON, M.A., Rev. W. F. ADENEY, M.A., Rev. A. F. MUIR, M.A., Rev. S. CONWAY, B.A., Rev. D. YOUNG, B.A. 15*s.*

Pulpit Commentary, The. (New Testament Series.)

St. Mark. By Very Rev. E. BICKERSTETH, D.D., Dean of Lichfield. With Homilies by Rev. Prof. THOMSON, M.A., Rev. Prof. GIVEN, M.A., Rev. Prof. JOHNSON, M.A., Rev. A. ROWLAND, B.A., LL.B., Rev. A. MUIR, and Rev. R. GREEN. Fifth Edition. 2 vols., 21*s.*

The Acts of the Apostles. By the Bishop of Bath and Wells. With Homilies by Rev. Prof. P. C. BARKER, M.A., LL.B., Rev. Prof. E. JOHNSON, M.A., Rev. Prof. R. A. REDFORD, M.A., Rev. R. TUCK, B.A., Rev. W. CLARKSON, B.A. Third Edition. 2 vols., 21*s.*

I. Corinthians. By the Ven. Archdeacon FARRAR, D.D. With Homilies by Rev. Ex-Chancellor LIPSCOMB, LL.D., Rev. DAVID THOMAS, D.D., Rev. D. FRASER, D.D., Rev. Prof. J. R. THOMSON, M.A., Rev. J. WAITE, B.A., Rev. R. TUCK, B.A., Rev. E. HURNDALL, M.A., and Rev. H. BREMNER, B.D. Third Edition. Price 15*s.*

II. Corinthians and Galatians. By the Ven. Archdeacon FARRAR, D.D., and Rev. Preb. E. HUXTABLE. With Homilies by Rev. Ex-Chancellor LIPSCOMB, LL.D., Rev. DAVID THOMAS, D.D., Rev. DONALD FRASER, D.D., Rev. R. TUCK, B.A., Rev. E. HURNDALL, M.A., Rev. Prof. J. R. THOMSON, M.A., Rev. R. FINLAYSON, B.A., Rev. W. F. ADENEY, M.A., Rev. R. M. EDGAR, M.A., and Rev. T. CROSKERRY, D.D. Price 21*s.*

Kegan Paul, Trench & Co.'s Publications. 25

Pulpit Commentary, The. (New Testament Series.)—*continued*.
Ephesians, Phillipians, and Colossians. By the Rev. Prof. W. G. BLAIKIE, D.D., Rev. B. C. CAFFIN, M.A., and Rev. G. G. FINDLAY, B.A. With Homilies by Rev. D. THOMAS, D.D., Rev. R. M. EDGAR, M.A., Rev. R. FINLAYSON, B.A., Rev. W. F. ADENEY, M.A., Rev. Prof. T. CROSKERRY, D.D., Rev. E. S. PROUT, M.A., Rev. Canon VERNON HUTTON, and Rev. U. R. THOMAS, D.D. Price 21s.

Hebrews and James. By the Rev. J. BARNBY, D.D., and Rev. Prebendary E. C. S. GIBSON, M.A. With Homiletics by the Rev. C. JERDAN, M.A., LL.B., and Rev. Prebendary E. C. S. GIBSON. And Homilies by the Rev. W. JONES, Rev. C. NEW, Rev. D. YOUNG, B.A., Rev. J. S. BRIGHT, Rev. T. F. LCCKYER, B.A., and Rev. C. JERDAN, M.A., LL.B. Price 15s.

PUNCHARD, E. G., D.D.—**Christ of Contention.** Three Essays. Fcap. 8vo, 2s.

PUSEY, Dr.—**Sermons for the Church's Seasons from Advent to Trinity.** Selected from the Published Sermons of the late EDWARD BOUVERIE PUSEY, D.D. Crown 8vo, 5s.

RANKE, Leopold von.—**Universal History.** The oldest Historical Group of Nations and the Greeks. Edited by G. W. PROTHERO. Demy 8vo, 16s.

RENDELL, J. M.—**Concise Handbook of the Island of Madeira.** With Plan of Funchal and Map of the Island. Fcap. 8vo, 1s. 6d.

REYNOLDS, Rev. J. W.—**The Supernatural in Nature.** A Verification by Free Use of Science. Third Edition, Revised and Enlarged. Demy 8vo, 14s.

The Mystery of Miracles. Third and Enlarged Edition. Crown 8vo, 6s.

The Mystery of the Universe; Our Common Faith. Demy 8vo, 14s.

RIBOT, Prof. Th.—**Heredity:** A Psychological Study on its Phenomena, its Laws, its Causes, and its Consequences. Second Edition. Large crown 8vo, 9s.

RIMMER, William, M.D.—**Art Anatomy.** A Portfolio of 81 Plates. Folio, 70s., nett.

ROBERTSON, The late Rev. F. W., M.A.—**Life and Letters of.** Edited by the Rev. STOPFORD BROOKE, M.A.
 I. Two vols., uniform with the Sermons. With Steel Portrait. Crown 8vo, 7s. 6d.
 II. Library Edition, in Demy 8vo, with Portrait. 12s.
 III. A Popular Edition, in 1 vol. Crown 8vo, 6s.

Sermons. Four Series. Small crown 8vo, 3s. 6d. each.

The Human Race, and other Sermons. Preached at Cheltenham, Oxford, and Brighton. New and Cheaper Edition. Small crown 8vo, 3s. 6d.

ROBERTSON, The late Rev. F. W., M.A.—continued.
>   Notes on Genesis. New and Cheaper Edition. Small crown 8vo, 3s. 6d.
>   Expository Lectures on St. Paul's Epistles to the Corinthians. A New Edition. Small crown 8vo, 5s.
>   Lectures and Addresses, with other Literary Remains. A New Edition. Small crown 8vo, 5s.
>   An Analysis of Tennyson's "In Memoriam." (Dedicated by Permission to the Poet-Laureate.) Fcap. 8vo, 2s.
>   The Education of the Human Race. Translated from the German of GOTTHOLD EPHRAIM LESSING. Fcap. 8vo, 2s. 6d.
>   The above Works can also be had, bound in half morocco.
>   *⁎* A Portrait of the late Rev. F. W. Robertson, mounted for framing, can be had, 2s. 6d.

ROMANES, G. J.—Mental Evolution in Animals. With a Posthumous Essay on Instinct by CHARLES DARWIN, F.R.S. Demy 8vo, 12s.

ROOSEVELT, Theodore. Hunting Trips of a Ranchman. Sketches of Sport on the Northern Cattle Plains. With 26 Illustrations. Royal 8vo, 18s.

Rosmini's Origin of Ideas. Translated from the Fifth Italian Edition of the Nuovo Saggio *Sull' origine delle idee.* 3 vols. Demy 8vo, cloth, 16s. each.

Rosmini's Psychology. 3 vols. Demy 8vo. [Vols. I. and II. now ready, 16s. each.

Rosmini's Philosophical System. Translated, with a Sketch of the Author's Life, Bibliography, Introduction, and Notes by THOMAS DAVIDSON. Demy 8vo, 16s.

RULE, Martin, M.A.—The Life and Times of St. Anselm, Archbishop of Canterbury and Primate of the Britains. 2 vols. Demy 8vo, 32s.

SAMUEL, Sydney M.—Jewish Life in the East. Small crown 8vo, 3s. 6d.

SARTORIUS, Ernestine.—Three Months in the Soudan. With 11 Full-page Illustrations. Demy 8vo, 14s.

SAYCE, Rev. Archibald Henry.—Introduction to the Science of Language. 2 vols. Second Edition. Large post 8vo, 21s.

SCOONES, W. Baptiste.—Four Centuries of English Letters: A Selection of 350 Letters by 150 Writers, from the Period of the Paston Letters to the Present Time. Third Edition. Large crown 8vo, 6s.

SÉE, Prof. Germain.—Bacillary Phthisis of the Lungs. Translated and edited for English Practitioners by WILLIAM HENRY WEDDELL, M.R.C.S. Demy 8vo, 10s. 6d.

Shakspere's Works. The Avon Edition, 12 vols., fcap. 8vo, cloth, 18s. ; in cloth box, 21s. ; bound in 6 vols., cloth, 15s.

SHILLITO, Rev. Joseph.—**Womanhood**: its Duties, Temptations, and Privileges. A Book for Young Women. Third Edition. Crown 8vo, 3s. 6d.

SIDNEY, Algernon.—A Review. By GERTRUDE M. IRELAND BLACKBURNE. Crown 8vo, 6s.

Sister Augustine, Superior of the Sisters of Charity at the St. Johannis Hospital at Bonn. Authorised Translation by HANS THARAU, from the German "Memorials of AMALIE VON LASAULX." Cheap Edition. Large crown 8vo, 4s. 6d.

SKINNER, James.—A Memoir. By the Author of "Charles Lowder." With a Preface by the Rev. Canon CARTER, and Portrait. Large crown, 7s. 6d.

⁎⁎⁎ Also a cheap Edition. With Portrait. Crown 8vo, 3s. 6d.

SMITH, Edward, M.D., LL.B., F.R.S.—**Tubercular Consumption in its Early and Remediable Stages.** Second Edition. Crown 8vo, 6s.

SMITH, Sir W. Cusack, Bart.—**Our War Ships.** A Naval Essay. Crown 8vo, 5s.

Spanish Mystics. By the Editor of "Many Voices." Crown 8vo, 5s.

Specimens of English Prose Style from Malory to Macaulay. Selected and Annotated, with an Introductory Essay, by GEORGE SAINTSBURY. Large crown 8vo, printed on handmade paper, parchment antique or cloth, 12s. ; vellum, 15s.

SPEDDING, James.—**Reviews and Discussions, Literary, Political, and Historical not relating to Bacon.** Demy 8vo, 12s. 6d.

Evenings with a Reviewer; or, Macaulay and Bacon. With a Prefatory Notice by G. S. VENABLES, Q.C. 2 vols. Demy 8vo, 18s.

STAPFER, Paul.—**Shakespeare and Classical Antiquity:** Greek and Latin Antiquity as presented in Shakespeare's Plays. Translated by EMILY J. CAREY. Large post 8vo, 12s.

STATHAM, F. Reginald.—**Free Thought and Truth Thought.** A Contribution to an Existing Argument. Crown 8vo, 6s.

STEVENSON, Rev. W. F.—**Hymns for the Church and Home.** Selected and Edited by the Rev. W. FLEMING STEVENSON.
The Hymn Book consists of Three Parts :—I. For Public Worship.—II. For Family and Private Worship.—III. For Children. SMALL EDITION. Cloth limp, 10d. ; cloth boards, 1s. LARGE TYPE EDITION. Cloth limp, 1s. 3d. ; cloth boards, 1s. 6d.

Stray Papers on Education, and Scenes from School Life. By B. H. Second Edition. Small crown 8vo, 3s. 6d.

STREATFEILD, Rev. G. S., M.A.—**Lincolnshire and the Danes.** Large crown 8vo, 7s. 6d.

STRECKER-WISLICENUS.—**Organic Chemistry.** Translated and Edited, with Extensive Additions, by W. R. HODGKINSON, Ph.D., and A. J. GREENAWAY, F.I.C. Second and cheaper Edition. Demy 8vo, 12s. 6d.

Suakin, 1885; being a Sketch of the Campaign of this year. By an Officer who was there. Second Edition. Crown 8vo, 2s. 6d.

SULLY, James, M.A.—**Pessimism :** a History and a Criticism. Second Edition. Demy 8vo, 14s.

Sunshine and Sea. A Yachting Visit to the Channel Islands and Coast of Brittany. With Frontispiece from a Photograph and 24 Illustrations. Crown 8vo, 6s.

SWEDENBORG, Eman.—**De Cultu et Amore Dei ubi Agitur de Telluris ortu, Paradiso et Vivario, tum de Primogeniti Seu Adami Nativitate Infantia, et Amore.** Crown 8vo, 6s.

On the Worship and Love of God. Treating of the Birth of the Earth, Paradise, and the Abode of Living Creatures. Translated from the original Latin. Crown 8vo, 7s. 6d.

Prodromus Philosophiæ Ratiocinantis de Infinito, et Causa Finali Creationis : deque Mechanismo Operationis Animæ et Corporis. Edidit THOMAS MURRAY GORMAN, M.A. Crown 8vo, 7s. 6d.

TACITUS.—**The Agricola.** A Translation. Small crown 8vo, 2s. 6d.

TAYLOR, Rev. Isaac.—**The Alphabet.** An Account of the Origin and Development of Letters. With numerous Tables and Facsimiles. 2 vols. Demy 8vo, 36s.

TAYLOR, Jeremy.—**The Marriage Ring.** With Preface, Notes, and Appendices. Edited by FRANCIS BURDETT MONEY COUTTS. Small crown 8vo, 2s. 6d.

TAYLOR, Sedley. — **Profit Sharing between Capital and Labour.** To which is added a Memorandum on the Industrial Partnership at the Whitwood Collieries, by ARCHIBALD and HENRY BRIGGS, with remarks by SEDLEY TAYLOR. Crown 8vo, 2s. 6d.

"They Might Have Been Together Till the Last." An Essay on Marriage, and the position of Women in England. Small crown 8vo, 2s.

Thirty Thousand Thoughts. Edited by the Rev. CANON SPENCE, Rev. J. S. EXELL, and Rev. CHARLES NEIL. 6 vols. Super royal 8vo.

[Vols. I.-IV. now ready, 16s. each.

THOM, J. Hamilton.—**Laws of Life after the Mind of Christ.** Two Series. Crown 8vo, 7s. 6d. each.

THOMPSON, Sir H.—**Diet in Relation to Age and Activity.** Fcap. 8vo, cloth, 1s. 6d.; Paper covers, 1s.

TIPPLE, Rev. S. A.—**Sunday Mornings at Norwood.** Prayers and Sermons. Crown 8vo, 6s.

TODHUNTER, Dr. J.—**A Study of Shelley.** Crown 8vo, 7s.

TOLSTOI, Count Leo.—**Christ's Christianity.** Translated from the Russian. Large crown 8vo, 7s. 6d.

TRANT, William.—**Trade Unions: Their Origin, Objects, and Efficacy.** Small crown 8vo, 1s. 6d.; paper covers, 1s.

TREMENHEERE, Hugh Seymour, C.B.—**A Manual of the Principles of Government,** as set forth by the Authorities of Ancient and Modern Times. New and Enlarged Edition. Crown 8vo, 3s. 6d. Cheap Edition, limp cloth, 1s.

TRENCH, The late R. C., Archbishop.—**Notes on the Parables of Our Lord.** Fourteenth Edition. 8vo, 12s.

Notes on the Miracles of Our Lord. Twelfth Edition. 8vo, 12s.

Studies in the Gospels. Fifth Edition, Revised. 8vo, 10s. 6d.

Brief Thoughts and Meditations on Some Passages in Holy Scripture. Third Edition. Crown 8vo, 3s. 6d.

Synonyms of the New Testament. Ninth Edition, Enlarged. 8vo, 12s.

Selected Sermons. Crown 8vo, 6s.

On the Authorized Version of the New Testament. Second Edition. 8vo, 7s.

Commentary on the Epistles to the Seven Churches in Asia. Fourth Edition, Revised. 8vo, 8s. 6d.

The Sermon on the Mount. An Exposition drawn from the Writings of St. Augustine, with an Essay on his Merits as an Interpreter of Holy Scripture. Fourth Edition, Enlarged. 8vo, 10s. 6d.

Shipwrecks of Faith. Three Sermons preached before the University of Cambridge in May, 1867. Fcap. 8vo, 2s. 6d.

Lectures on Mediæval Church History. Being the Substance of Lectures delivered at Queen's College, London. Second Edition. 8vo, 12s.

English, Past and Present. Thirteenth Edition, Revised and Improved. Fcap. 8vo, 5s.

On the Study of Words. Nineteenth Edition, Revised. Fcap. 8vo, 5s.

Select Glossary of English Words Used Formerly in Senses Different from the Present. Fifth Edition, Revised and Enlarged. Fcap. 8vo, 5s.

Proverbs and Their Lessons. Seventh Edition, Enlarged. Fcap. 8vo, 4s.

Poems. Collected and Arranged anew. Ninth Edition. Fcap. 8vo, 7s. 6d.

TRENCH, The late R. C., Archbishop.—continued.
  Poems. Library Edition. 2 vols. Small crown 8vo, 10s.
  Sacred Latin Poetry. Chiefly Lyrical, Selected and Arranged for Use. Third Edition, Corrected and Improved. Fcap. 8vo, 7s.
  A Household Book of English Poetry. Selected and Arranged, with Notes. Fourth Edition, Revised. Extra fcap. 8vo, 5s. 6d.
  An Essay on the Life and Genius of Calderon. With Translations from his "Life's a Dream" and "Great Theatre of the World." Second Edition, Revised and Improved. Extra fcap. 8vo, 5s. 6d.
  Gustavus Adolphus in Germany, and other Lectures on the Thirty Years' War. Second Edition, Enlarged. Fcap. 8vo, 4s.
  Plutarch: his Life, his Lives, and his Morals. Second Edition, Enlarged. Fcap. 8vo, 3s. 6d.
  Remains of the late Mrs. Richard Trench. Being Selections from her Journals, Letters, and other Papers. New and Cheaper Issue. With Portrait. 8vo, 6s.

TUKE, Daniel Hack, M.D., F.R.C.P.—**Chapters in the History of the Insane in the British Isles.** With Four Illustrations. Large crown 8vo, 12s.

TWINING, Louisa.—**Workhouse Visiting and Management during Twenty-Five Years.** Small crown 8vo, 2s.

TYLER, J.—**The Mystery of Being: or, What Do We Know?** Small crown 8vo, 3s. 6d.

VAUGHAN, H. Halford.—**New Readings and Renderings of Shakespeare's Tragedies.** 3 vols. Demy 8vo, 12s. 6d. each.

VILLARI, Professor.—**Niccolò Machiavelli and his Times.** Translated by LINDA VILLARI. 4 vols. Large post 8vo, 48s.

VILLIERS, The Right Hon. C. P.—**Free Trade Speeches of.** With Political Memoir. Edited by a Member of the Cobden Club. 2 vols. With Portrait. Demy 8vo, 25s.
  ‚ People's Edition. 1 vol. Crown 8vo, limp cloth, 2s. 6d.

VOGT, Lieut.-Col. Hermann.—**The Egyptian War of 1882.** A translation. With Map and Plans. Large crown 8vo, 6s.

VOLCKXSOM, E. W. v.—**Catechism of Elementary Modern Chemistry.** Small crown 8vo, 3s.

WALLER, Rev. C. B.—**The Apocalypse, reviewed under the Light of the Doctrine of the Unfolding Ages, and the Restitution of All Things.** Demy 8vo, 12s.
  The Bible Record of Creation viewed in its Letter and Spirit. Two Sermons preached at St. Paul's Church, Woodford Bridge. Crown 8vo, 1s. 6d.

Kegan Paul, Trench & Co.'s Publications. 31

WALPOLE, *Chas. George.*—A Short History of Ireland from the Earliest Times to the Union with Great Britain. With 5 Maps and Appendices. Second Edition. Crown 8vo, 6*s.*

WARD, *William George, Ph.D.*—Essays on the Philosophy of Theism. Edited, with an Introduction, by WILFRID WARD. 2 vols. Demy 8vo, 21*s.*

WARD, *Wilfrid.*—The Wish to Believe. A Discussion Concerning the Temper of Mind in which a reasonable Man should undertake Religious Inquiry. Small crown 8vo, 5*s.*

WARTER, *J. W.*—An Old Shropshire Oak. 2 vols. Demy 8vo, 28*s.*

WEDDERBURN, *Sir David, Bart., M.P.*—Life of. Compiled from his Journals and Writings by his sister, Mrs. E. H. PERCIVAL. With etched Portrait, and facsimiles of Pencil Sketches. Demy 8vo, 14*s.*

WEDMORE, *Frederick.*—The Masters of Genre Painting. With Sixteen Illustrations. Post 8vo, 7*s.* 6*d.*

WHITE, *R. E.*—Recollections of Woolwich during the Crimean War and Indian Mutiny, and of the Ordnance and War Departments; together with complete Lists of Past and Present Officials of the Royal Arsenal, etc. Crown 8vo, 2*s.* 6*d.*

WHITNEY, *Prof. William Dwight.*—Essentials of English Grammar, for the Use of Schools. Second Edition. Crown 8vo, 3*s.* 6*d.*

WHITWORTH, *George Clifford.*—An Anglo-Indian Dictionary: a Glossary of Indian Terms used in English, and of such English or other Non-Indian Terms as have obtained special meanings in India. Demy 8vo, cloth, 12*s.*

WILLIAMS, *Rowland, D.D.*—Psalms, Litanies, Counsels, and Collects for Devout Persons. Edited by his Widow. New and Popular Edition. Crown 8vo, 3*s.* 6*d.*

Stray Thoughts from the Note Books of the late Rowland Williams, D.D. Edited by his Widow. Crown 8vo, 3*s.* 6*d.*

WILSON, *Lieut.-Col. C. T.*—The Duke of Berwick, Marshal of France, 1702-1734. Demy 8vo, 15*s.*

WILSON, *Mrs. R. F.*—The Christian Brothers. Their Origin and Work. With a Sketch of the Life of their Founder, the Ven. JEAN BAPTISTE, de la Salle. Crown 8vo, 6*s.*

WOLTMANN, *Dr. Alfred, and* WOERMANN, *Dr. Karl.*—History of Painting. With numerous Illustrations. Vol. I. Painting in Antiquity and the Middle Ages. Medium 8vo, 28*s.*, bevelled boards, gilt leaves, 30*s.* Vol. II. The Painting of the Renascence.

YOUMANS, Eliza A.—**First Book of Botany.** Designed to Cultivate the Observing Powers of Children. With 300 Engravings. New and Cheaper Edition. Crown 8vo, 2s. 6d.

YOUMANS, Edward L., M.D.—**A Class Book of Chemistry**, on the Basis of the New System. With 200 Illustrations. Crown 8vo, 5s.

THE INTERNATIONAL SCIENTIFIC SERIES.

I. **Forms of Water**: a Familiar Exposition of the Origin and Phenomena of Glaciers. By J. Tyndall, LL.D., F.R.S. With 25 Illustrations. Ninth Edition. 5s.

II. **Physics and Politics**; or, Thoughts on the Application of the Principles of "Natural Selection" and "Inheritance" to Political Society. By Walter Bagehot. Seventh Edition. 4s.

III. **Foods.** By Edward Smith, M.D., LL.B., F.R.S. With numerous Illustrations. Eighth Edition. 5s.

IV. **Mind and Body**: the Theories of their Relation. By Alexander Bain, LL.D. With Four Illustrations. Seventh Edition. 4s.

V. **The Study of Sociology.** By Herbert Spencer. Twelfth Edition. 5s.

VI. **On the Conservation of Energy.** By Balfour Stewart, M.A., LL.D., F.R.S. With 14 Illustrations. Sixth Edition. 5s.

VII. **Animal Locomotion**; or Walking, Swimming, and Flying. By J. B. Pettigrew, M.D., F.R.S., etc. With 130 Illustrations. Third Edition. 5s.

VIII. **Responsibility in Mental Disease.** By Henry Maudsley, M.D. Fourth Edition. 5s.

IX. **The New Chemistry.** By Professor J. P. Cooke. With 31 Illustrations. Eighth Edition, remodelled and enlarged. 5s.

X. **The Science of Law.** By Professor Sheldon Amos. Sixth Edition. 5s.

XI. **Animal Mechanism**: a Treatise on Terrestrial and Aerial Locomotion. By Professor E. J. Marey. With 117 Illustrations. Third Edition. 5s.

XII. **The Doctrine of Descent and Darwinism.** By Professor Oscar Schmidt. With 26 Illustrations. Sixth Edition. 5s.

XIII. **The History of the Conflict between Religion and Science.** By J. W. Draper, M.D., LL.D. Nineteenth Edition. 5s.

XIV. **Fungi**: their Nature, Influences, Uses, etc. By M. C. Cooke, M.D., LL.D. Edited by the Rev. M. J. Berkeley, M.A., F.L.S. With numerous Illustrations. Third Edition. 5s.

Kegan Paul, Trench & Co.'s Publications. 33

XV. **The Chemical Effects of Light and Photography.** By Dr. Hermann Vogel. With 100 Illustrations. Fourth Edition. 5s.
XVI. **The Life and Growth of Language.** By Professor William Dwight Whitney. Fifth Edition. 5s.
XVII. **Money and the Mechanism of Exchange.** By W. Stanley Jevons, M.A., F.R.S. Seventh Edition. 5s.
XVIII. **The Nature of Light.** With a General Account of Physical Optics. By Dr. Eugene Lommel. With 188 Illustrations and a Table of Spectra in Chromo-lithography. Third Edition. 5s.
XIX. **Animal Parasites and Messmates.** By P. J. Van Beneden. With 83 Illustrations. Third Edition. 5s.
XX. **Fermentation.** By Professor Schützenberger. With 28 Illustrations. Fourth Edition. 5s.
XXI. **The Five Senses of Man.** By Professor Bernstein. With 91 Illustrations. Fifth Edition. 5s.
XXII. **The Theory of Sound in its Relation to Music.** By Professor Pietro Blaserna. With numerous Illustrations. Third Edition. 5s.
XXIII. **Studies in Spectrum Analysis.** By J. Norman Lockyer, F.R.S. With six photographic Illustrations of Spectra, and numerous engravings on Wood. Third Edition. 6s. 6d.
XXIV. **A History of the Growth of the Steam Engine.** By Professor R. H. Thurston. With numerous Illustrations. Third Edition. 6s. 6d.
XXV. **Education as a Science.** By Alexander Bain, LL.D. Fifth Edition. 5s.
XXVI. **The Human Species.** By Professor A. de Quatrefages. Third Edition. 5s.
XXVII. **Modern Chromatics.** With Applications to Art and Industry. By Ogden N. Rood. With 130 original Illustrations. Second Edition. 5s.
XXVIII. **The Crayfish:** an Introduction to the Study of Zoology. By Professor T. H. Huxley. With 82 Illustrations. Fourth Edition. 5s.
XXIX. **The Brain as an Organ of Mind.** By H. Charlton Bastian, M.D. With numerous Illustrations. Third Edition. 5s.
XXX. **The Atomic Theory.** By Prof. Wurtz. Translated by G. Cleminshaw, F.C.S. Fourth Edition. 5s.
XXXI. **The Natural Conditions of Existence as they affect Animal Life.** By Karl Semper. With 2 Maps and 106 Woodcuts. Third Edition. 5s.
XXXII. **General Physiology of Muscles and Nerves.** By Prof. J. Rosenthal. Third Edition. With Illustrations. 5s.

D

XXXIII. **Sight:** an Exposition of the Principles of Monocular and Binocular Vision. By Joseph le Conte, LL.D. Second Edition. With 132 Illustrations. 5s.

XXXIV. **Illusions:** a Psychological Study. By James Sully. Second Edition. 5s.

XXXV. **Volcanoes: what they are and what they teach.** By Professor J. W. Judd, F.R.S. With 92 Illustrations on Wood. Third Edition. 5s.

XXXVI. **Suicide:** an Essay on Comparative Moral Statistics. By Prof. H. Morselli. Second Edition. With Diagrams. 5s.

XXXVII. **The Brain and its Functions.** By J. Luys. With Illustrations. Second Edition. 5s.

XXXVIII. **Myth and Science:** an Essay. By Tito Vignoli. Second Edition. 5s.

XXXIX. **The Sun.** By Professor Young. With Illustrations. Second Edition. 5s.

XL. **Ants, Bees, and Wasps:** a Record of Observations on the Habits of the Social Hymenoptera. By Sir John Lubbock, Bart., M.P. With 5 Chromo-lithographic Illustrations. Eighth Edition. 5s.

XLI. **Animal Intelligence.** By G. J. Romanes, LL.D., F.R.S. Third Edition. 5s.

XLII. **The Concepts and Theories of Modern Physics.** By J. B. Stallo. Third Edition. 5s.

XLIII. **Diseases of the Memory;** An Essay in the Positive Psychology. By Prof. Th. Ribot. Second Edition. 5s.

XLIV. **Man before Metals.** By N. Joly, with 148 Illustrations. Third Edition. 5s.

XLV. **The Science of Politics.** By Prof. Sheldon Amos. Third Edition. 5s.

XLVI. **Elementary Meteorology.** By Robert H. Scott. Third Edition. With Numerous Illustrations. 5s.

XLVII. **The Organs of Speech and their Application in the Formation of Articulate Sounds.** By Georg Hermann Von Meyer. With 47 Woodcuts. 5s.

XLVIII. **Fallacies.** A View of Logic from the Practical Side. By Alfred Sidgwick. 5s.

XLIX. **Origin of Cultivated Plants.** By Alphonse de Candolle. 5s.

L. **Jelly-Fish, Star-Fish, and Sea-Urchins.** Being a Research on Primitive Nervous Systems. By G. J. Romanes. With Illustrations. 5s.

LI. **The Common Sense of the Exact Sciences.** By the late William Kingdon Clifford. Second Edition. With 100 Figures. 5s.

LII. **Physical Expression: Its Modes and Principles.** By Francis Warner, M.D., F.R.C.P. With 50 Illustrations. 5s.

LIII. **Anthropoid Apes.** By Robert Hartmann. With 63 Illustrations. 5s.

LIV. **The Mammalia in their Relation to Primeval Times.** By Oscar Schmidt. With 51 Woodcuts. 5s.

LV. **Comparative Literature.** By H. Macaulay Posnett, LL.D. 5s.

LVI. **Earthquakes and other Earth Movements.** By Prof. JOHN MILNE. With 38 Figures. 5s.

LVII. **Microbes, Ferments, and Moulds.** By E. L. TROUESSART. With 107 Illustrations. 5s.

MILITARY WORKS.

BRACKENBURY, Col. C. B., R.A.—**Military Handbooks for Regimental Officers.**

I. **Military Sketching and Reconnaissance.** By Col. F. J. Hutchison and Major H. G. MacGregor. Fourth Edition. With 15 Plates. Small crown 8vo, 4s.

II. **The Elements of Modern Tactics Practically applied to English Formations.** By Lieut.-Col. Wilkinson Shaw. Fifth Edition. With 25 Plates and Maps. Small crown 8vo, 9s.

III. **Field Artillery.** Its Equipment, Organization and Tactics. By Major Sisson C. Pratt, R.A. With 12 Plates. Second Edition. Small crown 8vo, 6s.

IV. **The Elements of Military Administration.** First Part: Permanent System of Administration. By Major J. W. Buxton. Small crown 8vo. 7s. 6d.

V. **Military Law:** Its Procedure and Practice. By Major Sisson C. Pratt, R.A. Second Edition. Small crown 8vo, 4s. 6d.

VI. **Cavalry in Modern War.** By Col. F. Chenevix Trench. Small crown 8vo, 6s.

VII. **Field Works.** Their Technical Construction and Tactical Application. By the Editor, Col. C. B. Brackenbury, R.A. Small crown 8vo.

BRENT, Brig.-Gen. J. L.—**Mobilizable Fortifications and their Controlling Influence in War.** Crown 8vo, 5s.

BROOKE, Major, C. K.—**A System of Field Training.** Small crown 8vo, cloth limp, 2s.

CLERY, C., Lieut.-Col.—**Minor Tactics.** With 26 Maps and Plans. Seventh Edition, Revised. Crown 8vo, 9s.

COLVILE, Lieut.-Col. C. F.—**Military Tribunals.** Sewed, 2s. 6d.

CRAUFURD, Capt. H. J.—**Suggestions for the Military Training of a Company of Infantry.** Crown 8vo, 1s. 6d.

HAMILTON, Capt. Ian, A.D.C.—**The Fighting of the Future.** 1s.

HARRISON, Col. R.—**The Officer's Memorandum Book for Peace and War.** Fourth Edition, Revised throughout. Oblong 32mo, red basil, with pencil, 3s. 6d.

Notes on Cavalry Tactics, Organisation, etc. By a Cavalry Officer. With Diagrams. Demy 8vo, 12s.

PARR, Capt. H. Hallam, C.M.G.—**The Dress, Horses, and Equipment of Infantry and Staff Officers.** Crown 8vo, 1s.

SCHAW, Col. H.—**The Defence and Attack of Positions and Localities.** Third Edition, Revised and Corrected. Crown 8vo, 3s. 6d.

STONE, Capt. F. Gleadowe, R.A.—**Tactical Studies from the Franco-German War of 1870–71.** With 22 Lithographic Sketches and Maps. Demy 8vo, 30s.

WILKINSON, H. Spenser, Capt. 20th Lancashire R.V.—**Citizen Soldiers.** Essays towards the Improvement of the Volunteer Force. Crown 8vo, 2s. 6d.

POETRY.

ADAM OF ST. VICTOR.—**The Liturgical Poetry of Adam of St. Victor.** From the text of GAUTIER. With Translations into English in the Original Metres, and Short Explanatory Notes, by DIGBY S. WRANGHAM, M.A. 3 vols. Crown 8vo, printed on hand-made paper, boards, 21s.

AUCHMUTY, A. C.—**Poems of English Heroism:** From Brunanburh to Lucknow; from Athelstan to Albert. Small crown 8vo, 1s. 6d.

BARNES, William.—**Poems of Rural Life, in the Dorset Dialect.** New Edition, complete in one vol. Crown 8vo, 8s. 6d.

BAYNES, Rev. Canon H. R.—**Home Songs for Quiet Hours.** Fourth and Cheaper Edition. Fcap. 8vo, cloth, 2s. 6d.

BEVINGTON, L. S.—**Key Notes.** Small crown 8vo, 5s.

BLUNT, Wilfrid Scawen.—**The Wind and the Whirlwind.** Demy 8vo, 1s. 6d.

BLUNT, *Wilfred Scawen—continued.*
 The Love Sonnets of Proteus. Fifth Edition, 18mo. Cloth extra, gilt top, 5s.

BOWEN, H. C., M.A.—**Simple English Poems.** English Literature for Junior Classes. In Four Parts. Parts I., II., and III., 6d. each, and Part IV., 1s. Complete, 3s.

BRYANT, W. C.—**Poems.** Cheap Edition, with Frontispiece. Small crown 8vo, 3s. 6d.

Calderon's Dramas: the Wonder-Working Magician — Life is a Dream—the Purgatory of St. Patrick. Translated by DENIS FLORENCE MACCARTHY. Post 8vo, 10s.

Camoens Lusiads. — Portuguese Text, with Translation by J. J. AUBERTIN. Second Edition. 2 vols. Crown 8vo, 12s.

CAMPBELL, *Lewis.*—Sophocles. The Seven Plays in English Verse. Crown 8vo, 7s. 6d.

CERVANTES.—Journey to Parnassus. Spanish Text, with Translation into English Tercets, Preface, and Illustrative Notes, by JAMES Y. GIBSON. Crown 8vo, 12s.

 Numantia: a Tragedy. Translated from the Spanish, with Introduction and Notes, by JAMES Y. GIBSON. Crown 8vo, printed on hand-made paper, 5s.

CHAVANNES, *Mary Charlotte.* — **A Few Translations from Victor Hugo and other Poets.** Small crown 8vo, 2s. 6d.

CHRISTIE, A. J.—**The End of Man.** With 4 Autotype Illustrations. 4to, 10s. 6d.

Chronicles of Christopher Columbus. A Poem in 12 Cantos. By M. D. C. Crown 8vo, 7s. 6d.

CLARKE, *Mary Cowden.*—Honey from the Weed. Verses. Crown 8vo, 7s.

COXHEAD, *Ethel.*—Birds and Babies. Imp. 16mo. With 33 Illustrations. Gilt, 2s. 6d.

DE BERANGER.—A Selection from his Songs. In English Verse. By WILLIAM TOYNBEE. Small crown 8vo, 2s. 6d.

DENNIS, J.—English Sonnets. Collected and Arranged by. Small crown 8vo, 2s. 6d.

DE VERE, *Aubrey.*—Poetical Works.
 I. THE SEARCH AFTER PROSERPINE, etc. 6s.
 II. THE LEGENDS OF ST. PATRICK, etc. 6s.
 III. ALEXANDER THE GREAT, etc. 6s.

 The Foray of Queen Meave, and other Legends of Ireland's Heroic Age. Small crown 8vo, 5s.

 Legends of the Saxon Saints. Small crown 8vo, 6s.

DOBSON, Austin.—Old World Idylls and other Verses. Sixth Edition. Elzevir 8vo, gilt top, 6*s.*
    At the Sign of the Lyre. Fourth Edition. Elzevir 8vo, gilt top, 6*s.*
DOMETT, Alfred.—Ranolf and Amohia. A Dream of Two Lives. New Edition, Revised. 2 vols. Crown 8vo, 12*s.*
Dorothy : a Country Story in Elegiac Verse. With Preface. Demy 8vo, 5*s.*
DOWDEN, Edward, LL.D.—Shakspere's Sonnets. With Introduction and Notes. Large post 8vo, 7*s.* 6*d.*
Dulce Cor : being the Poems of Ford Berêton. With Two Illustrations. Crown 8vo, 6*s.*
DUTT, Toru.—A Sheaf Gleaned in French Fields. New Edition. Demy 8vo, 10*s.* 6*d.*
    Ancient Ballads and Legends of Hindustan. With an Introductory Memoir by EDMUND GOSSE. Second Edition, 18mo. Cloth extra, gilt top, 5*s.*
EDWARDS, Miss Betham.—Poems. Small crown 8vo, 3*s.* 6*d.*
ELDRYTH, Maud.—Margaret, and other Poems. Small crown 8vo, 3*s.* 6*d.*
    All Soul's Eve, "No God," and other Poems. Fcap. 8vo, 3*s.* 6*d.*
ELLIOTT, Ebenezer, The Corn Law Rhymer.—Poems. Edited by his son, the Rev. EDWIN ELLIOTT, of St. John's, Antigua. 2 vols. Crown 8vo, 18*s.*
English Verse. Edited by W. J. LINTON and R. H. STODDARD. 5 vols. Crown 8vo, cloth, 5*s.* each.
    I. CHAUCER TO BURNS.
    II. TRANSLATIONS.
    III. LYRICS OF THE NINETEENTH CENTURY.
    IV. DRAMATIC SCENES AND CHARACTERS.
    V. BALLADS AND ROMANCES.
ENIS.—Gathered Leaves. Small crown 8vo, 3*s.* 6*d.*
EVANS, Anne.—Poems and Music. With Memorial Preface by ANN THACKERAY RITCHIE. Large crown 8vo, 7*s.*
GOODCHILD, John A.—Somnia Medici. Two series. Small crown 8vo, 5*s.* each.
GOSSE, Edmund W.—New Poems. Crown 8vo, 7*s.* 6*d.*
    Firdausi in Exile, and other Poems. Elzevir 8vo, gilt top, 6*s.*
GRINDROD, Charles.—Plays from English History. Crown 8vo, 7*s.* 6*d.*
    The Stranger's Story, and his Poem, The Lament of Love : An Episode of the Malvern Hills. Small crown 8vo, 2*s.* 6*d.*

GURNEY, *Rev. Alfred.*—The Vision of the Eucharist, and other Poems. Crown 8vo, 5*s.*

A Christmas Faggot. Small crown 8vo, 5*s.*

HENRY, *Daniel, Junr.*—Under a Fool's Cap. Songs. Crown 8vo, cloth, bevelled boards, 5*s.*

HEYWOOD, *J. C.*—Herodias, a Dramatic Poem. New Edition, Revised. Small crown 8vo, 5*s.*

Antonius. A Dramatic Poem. New Edition, Revised. Small crown 8vo, 5*s.*

HICKEY, *E. H.*—A Sculptor, and other Poems. Small crown 8vo, 5*s.*

HOLE, *W. G.*—Procris, and other Poems. Fcap. 8vo, 3*s.* 6*d.*

KEATS, *John.*—Poetical Works. Edited by W. T. ARNOLD. Large crown 8vo, choicely printed on hand-made paper, with Portrait in *eau-forte.* Parchment or cloth, 12*s.*; vellum, 15*s.*

KING, *Mrs. Hamilton.*—The Disciples. Eighth Edition, and Notes. Small crown 8vo, 5*s.*

A Book of Dreams. Crown 8vo, 3*s.* 6*d.*

KNOX, *The Hon. Mrs. O. N.*—Four Pictures from a Life, and other Poems. Small crown 8vo, 3*s.* 6*d.*

LANG, *A.*—XXXII Ballades in Blue China. Elzevir 8vo, 5*s.*

Rhymes à la Mode. With Frontispiece by E. A. Abbey. Elzevir 8vo, cloth extra, gilt top, 5*s.*

LAWSON, *Right Hon. Mr. Justice.*—Hymni Usitati Latine Redditi: with other Verses. Small 8vo, parchment, 5*s.*

Lessing's Nathan the Wise. Translated by EUSTACE K. CORBETT. Crown 8vo, 6*s.*

Life Thoughts. Small crown 8vo, 2*s.* 6*d.*

Living English Poets MDCCCLXXXII. With Frontispiece by Walter Crane. Second Edition. Large crown 8vo. Printed on hand-made paper. Parchment or cloth, 12*s.*; vellum, 15*s.*

LOCKER, *F.*—London Lyrics. Tenth Edition. With Portrait, Elzevir 8vo. Cloth extra, gilt top, 5*s.*

Love in Idleness. A Volume of Poems. With an Etching by W. B. Scott. Small crown 8vo, 5*s.*

LUMSDEN, *Lieut.-Col. H. W.*—Beowulf: an Old English Poem. Translated into Modern Rhymes. Second and Revised Edition. Small crown 8vo, 5*s.*

LYSAGHT, *Sidney Royse.*—A Modern Ideal. A Dramatic Poem. Small crown 8vo, 5*s.*

MACGREGOR, *Duncan.*—Clouds and Sunlight. Poems. Small crown 8vo, 5*s.*

MAGNUSSON, Eirikr, M.A., and PALMER, E. H., M.A.—Johan Ludvig Runeberg's Lyrical Songs, Idylls, and Epigrams. Fcap. 8vo, 5s.

MAKCLOUD, Even.—Ballads of the Western Highlands and Islands of Scotland. Small crown 8vo, 3s. 6d.

MC'NAUGHTON, J. H.—Onnalinda. A Romance. Small crown 8vo, 7s. 6d.

MEREDITH, Owen [*The Earl of Lytton*].—Lucile. New Edition. With 32 Illustrations. 16mo, 3s. 6d. Cloth extra, gilt edges, 4s. 6d.

MORRIS, Lewis.—Poetical Works of. New and Cheaper Editions, with Portrait. Complete in 3 vols., 5s. each.
Vol. I. contains "Songs of Two Worlds." Eleventh Edition.
Vol. II. contains "The Epic of Hades." Twentieth Edition.
Vol. III. contains "Gwen" and "The Ode of Life." Sixth Edition.

The Epic of Hades. With 16 Autotype Illustrations, after the Drawings of the late George R. Chapman. 4to, cloth extra, gilt leaves, 21s.

The Epic of Hades. Presentation Edition. 4to, cloth extra, gilt leaves, 10s. 6d.

Songs Unsung. Fifth Edition. Fcap. 8vo, 5s.

The Lewis Morris Birthday Book. Edited by S. S. COPEMAN, with Frontispiece after a Design by the late George R. Chapman. 32mo, cloth extra, gilt edges, 2s.; cloth limp, 1s. 6d.

MORSHEAD, E. D. A.—The House of Atreus. Being the Agamemnon, Libation-Bearers, and Furies of Æschylus. Translated into English Verse. Crown 8vo, 7s.

The Suppliant Maidens of Æschylus. Crown 8vo, 3s. 6d.

MOZLEY, J. Rickards.—The Romance of Dennell. A Poem in Five Cantos. Crown 8vo, 7s. 6d.

MULHOLLAND, Rosa.—Vagrant Verses. Small crown 8vo, 5s.

NOEL, The Hon. Roden.—A Little Child's Monument. Third Edition. Small crown 8vo, 3s. 6d.

The House of Ravensburg. New Edition. Small crown 8vo, 6s.

The Red Flag, and other Poems. New Edition. Small crown 8vo, 6s.

Songs of the Heights and Deeps. Crown 8vo, 6s.

OBBARD, Constance Mary.—Burley Bells. Small crown 8vo, 3s. 6d.

O'HAGAN, John.—The Song of Roland. Translated into English Verse. New and Cheaper Edition. Crown 8vo, 5s.

PFEIFFER, Emily.—The Rhyme of the Lady of the Rock, and How it Grew. Second Edition. Small crown 8vo, 3s. 6d.

PFEIFFER, *Emily—continued.*
    Gerard's Monument, and other Poems. Second Edition. Crown 8vo, 6s.
    Under the Aspens: Lyrical and Dramatic. With Portrait. Crown 8vo, 6s.

PIATT, *J. J.*—Idyls and Lyrics of the Ohio Valley. Crown 8vo, 5s.

PIATT, *Sarah M. B.*—A Voyage to the Fortunate Isles, and other Poems. 1 vol. Small crown 8vo, gilt top, 5s.
    In Primrose Time. A New Irish Garland. Small crown 8vo, 2s. 6d.

Rare Poems of the 16th and 17th Centuries. Edited W. J. LINTON. Crown 8vo, 5s.

RHOADES, *James.*—The Georgics of Virgil. Translated into English Verse. Small crown 8vo, 5s.
    Poems. Small crown 8vo, 4s. 6d.

ROBINSON, *A. Mary F.*—A Handful of Honeysuckle. Fcap. 8vo, 3s. 6d.
    The Crowned Hippolytus. Translated from Euripides. With New Poems. Small crown 8vo, 5s.

ROUS, *Lieut.-Col.*—Conradin. Small crown 8vo, 2s.

SANDYS, *R. H.*—Egeus, and other Poems. Small crown 8vo, 3s. 6d.

SCHILLER, *Friedrich.*—Wallenstein. A Drama. Done in English Verse, by J. A. W. HUNTER, M.A. Crown 8vo, 7s. 6d.

SCOTT, *E. J. L.*—The Eclogues of Virgil.—Translated into English Verse. Small crown 8vo, 3s. 6d.

SCOTT, *George F. E.*—Theodora and other Poems. Small crown 8vo, 3s. 6d.

SEYMOUR, *F. H. A.*—Rienzi. A Play in Five Acts. Small crown 8vo, 5s.

Shakspere's Works. The Avon Edition, 12 vols., fcap. 8vo, cloth, 18s.; and in box, 21s.; bound in 6 vols., cloth, 15s.

SHERBROOKE, *Viscount.*—Poems of a Life. Second Edition. Small crown 8vo, 2s. 6d.

SMITH, *J. W. Gilbart.*—The Loves of Vandyck. A Tale of Genoa. Small crown 8vo, 2s. 6d.
    The Log o' the "Norseman." Small crown 8vo, 5s.

Songs of Coming Day. Small crown 8vo, 3s. 6d.

Sophocles: The Seven Plays in English Verse. Translated by LEWIS CAMPBELL. Crown 8vo, 7s. 6d.

SPICER, *Henry.*—Haska: a Drama in Three Acts (as represented at the Theatre Royal, Drury Lane, March 10th, 1877). Third Edition. Crown 8vo, 3s. 6d.
    Uriel Acosta, in Three Acts. From the German of Gatzkow. Small crown 8vo, 2s. 6d.

SYMONDS, *John Addington.*—**Vagabunduli Libellus.** Crown 8vo, 6s.

Tasso's Jerusalem Delivered. Translated by Sir JOHN KINGSTON JAMES, Bart. Two Volumes. Printed on hand-made paper, parchment, bevelled boards. Large crown 8vo, 21s.

TAYLOR, *Sir H.*—**Works.** Complete in Five Volumes. Crown 8vo, 30s.
    Philip Van Artevelde. Fcap. 8vo, 3s. 6d.
    The Virgin Widow, etc. Fcap. 8vo, 3s. 6d.
    The Statesman. Fcap. 8vo, 3s. 6d.

TAYLOR, *Augustus.*—**Poems.** Fcap. 8vo, 5s.

TAYLOR, *Margaret Scott.*—"**Boys Together,**" and other Poems. Small crown 8vo, 6s.

TODHUNTER, *Dr. J.*—**Laurella, and other Poems.** Crown 8vo, 6s. 6d.
    Forest Songs. Small crown 8vo, 3s. 6d.
    The True Tragedy of Rienzi: a Drama. 3s. 6d.
    Alcestis: a Dramatic Poem. Extra fcap. 8vo, 5s.
    Helena in Troas. Small crown 8vo, 2s. 6d.

TYLER, *M. C.*—**Anne Boleyn.** A Tragedy in Six Acts. Second Edition. Small crown 8vo, 2s. 6d.

TYNAN, *Katherine.*—**Louise de la Valliere, and other Poems.** Small crown 8vo, 3s. 6d.

WEBSTER, *Augusta.*—**In a Day:** a Drama. Small crown 8vo, 2s. 6d.
    Disguises: a Drama. Small crown 8vo, 5s.

Wet Days. By a Farmer. Small crown 8vo, 6s.

WOOD, *Rev. F. H.*—**Echoes of the Night, and other Poems.** Small crown 8vo, 3s. 6d.

Wordsworth Birthday Book, The. Edited by ADELAIDE and VIOLET WORDSWORTH. 32mo, limp cloth, 1s. 6d.; cloth extra, 2s.

YOUNGMAN, *Thomas George.*—**Poems.** Small crown 8vo, 5s.

YOUNGS, *Ella Sharpe.*—**Paphus, and other Poems.** Small crown 8vo, 3s. 6d.
    A Heart's Life, Sarpedon, and other Poems. Small crown 8vo, 3s. 6d.

NOVELS AND TALES.

"**All But:**" a Chronicle of Laxenford Life. By PEN OLIVER, F.R.C.S. With 20 Illustrations. Second Edition. Crown 8vo, 6s.

BANKS, *Mrs. G. L.*—**God's Providence House.** New Edition. Crown 8vo, 3s. 6d.

CHICHELE, *Mary.*—**Doing and Undoing.** A Story. Crown 8vo, 4s. 6d.

Danish Parsonage. By an Angler. Crown 8vo, 6s.

Kegan Paul, Trench & Co.'s Publications. 43

HUNTER, *Hay.*—**The Crime of Christmas Day.** A Tale of the Latin Quarter. By the Author of "My Ducats and my Daughter." 1s.
HUNTER, *Hay, and* WHYTE, *Walter.*—**My Ducats and My Daughter.** New and Cheaper Edition. With Frontispiece. Crown 8vo, 6s.
Hurst and Hanger. A History in Two Parts. 3 vols. 31s. 6d.
INGELOW, *Jean.*—**Off the Skelligs**: a Novel. With Frontispiece. Second Edition. Crown 8vo, 6s.
JENKINS, *Edward.*—**A Secret of Two Lives.** Crown 8vo, 2s. 6d.
KIELLAND, *Alexander L.*—**Garman and Worse.** A Norwegian Novel. Authorized Translation, by W. W. Kettlewell. Crown 8vo, 6s.
MACDONALD, *G.*—**Donal Grant.** A Novel. Second Edition. With Frontispiece. Crown 8vo, 6s.
  Castle Warlock. A Novel. Second Edition. With Frontispiece. Crown 8vo, 6s.
  Malcolm. With Portrait of the Author engraved on Steel. Seventh Edition. Crown 8vo, 6s.
  The Marquis of Lossie. Sixth Edition. With Frontispiece. Crown 8vo, 6s.
  St. George and St. Michael. Fifth Edition. With Frontispiece. Crown 8vo, 6s.
  What's Mine's Mine. Second Edition. With Frontispiece. Crown 8vo, 6s.
  Annals of a Quiet Neighbourhood. Fifth Edition. With Frontispiece. Crown 8vo, 6s.
  The Seaboard Parish: a Sequel to "Annals of a Quiet Neighbourhood." Fourth Edition. With Frontispiece. Crown 8vo, 6s.
  Wilfred Cumbermede. An Autobiographical Story. Fourth Edition. With Frontispiece. Crown 8vo, 6s.
MALET, *Lucas.*—**Colonel Enderby's Wife.** A Novel. New and Cheaper Edition. With Frontispiece. Crown 8vo, 6s.
MULHOLLAND, *Rosa.*—**Marcella Grace.** An Irish Novel. Crown 8vo.
PALGRAVE, *W. Gifford.*—**Hermann Agha**: an Eastern Narrative. Third Edition. Crown 8vo, 6s.
SHAW, *Flora L.*—**Castle Blair**: a Story of Youthful Days. New and Cheaper Edition. Crown 8vo, 3s. 6d.
STRETTON, *Hesba.*—**Through a Needle's Eye**: a Story. New and Cheaper Edition, with Frontispiece. Crown 8vo, 6s.
TAYLOR, *Col. Meadows, C.S.I., M.R.I.A.*—**Seeta**: a Novel. With Frontispiece. Crown 8vo, 6s.
  Tippoo Sultaun: a Tale of the Mysore War. With Frontispiece. Crown 8vo, 6s.
  Ralph Darnell. With Frontispiece. Crown 8vo, 6s.
  A Noble Queen. With Frontispiece. Crown 8vo, 6s.
  The Confessions of a Thug. With Frontispiece. Crown 8vo, 6s.
  Tara: a Mahratta Tale. With Frontispiece. Crown 8vo, 6s.
Within Sound of the Sea. With Frontispiece. Crown 8vo, 6s.

BOOKS FOR THE YOUNG.

Brave Men's Footsteps. A Book of Example and Anecdote for Young People. By the Editor of "Men who have Risen." With 4 Illustrations by C. Doyle. Eighth Edition. Crown 8vo, 3*s.* 6*d.*

COXHEAD, *Ethel.*—**Birds and Babies.** Imp. 16mo. With 33 Illustrations. Cloth gilt, 2*s.* 6*d.*

DAVIES, *G. Christopher.*—**Rambles and Adventures of our School Field Club.** With 4 Illustrations. New and Cheaper Edition. Crown 8vo, 3*s.* 6*d.*

EDMONDS, *Herbert.*—**Well Spent Lives:** a Series of Modern Biographies. New and Cheaper Edition. Crown 8vo, 3*s.* 6*d.*

EVANS, *Mark.*—**The Story of our Father's Love**, told to Children. Sixth and Cheaper Edition of Theology for Children. With 4 Illustrations. Fcap. 8vo, 1*s.* 6*d.*

JOHNSON, *Virginia W.*—**The Catskill Fairies.** Illustrated by Alfred Fredericks. 5*s.*

MAC KENNA, *S. J.*—**Plucky Fellows.** A Book for Boys. With 6 Illustrations. Fifth Edition. Crown 8vo, 3*s.* 6*d.*

REANEY, *Mrs. G. S.*—**Waking and Working**; or, From Girlhood to Womanhood. New and Cheaper Edition. With a Frontispiece. Crown 8vo, 3*s.* 6*d.*

Blessing and Blessed: a Sketch of Girl Life. New and Cheaper Edition. Crown 8vo, 3*s.* 6*d.*

Rose Gurney's Discovery. A Story for Girls. Dedicated to their Mothers. Crown 8vo, 3*s.* 6*d.*

English Girls: Their Place and Power. With Preface by the Rev. R. W. Dale. Fourth Edition. Fcap. 8vo, 2*s.* 6*d.*

Just Anyone, and other Stories. Three Illustrations. Royal 16mo, 1*s.* 6*d.*

Sunbeam Willie, and other Stories. Three Illustrations. Royal 16mo, 1*s.* 6*d.*

Sunshine Jenny, and other Stories. Three Illustrations. Royal 16mo, 1*s.* 6*d.*

STOCKTON, *Frank R.*—**A Jolly Fellowship.** With 20 Illustrations. Crown 8vo, 5*s.*

STORR, *Francis, and* TURNER, *Hawes.*—**Canterbury Chimes;** or, Chaucer Tales re-told to Children. With 6 Illustrations from the Ellesmere Manuscript. Third Edition. Fcap. 8vo, 3*s.* 6*d.*

STRETTON, *Hesba.*—**David Lloyd's Last Will.** With 4 Illustrations. New Edition. Royal 16mo, 2*s.* 6*d.*

WHITAKER, *Florence.*—**Christy's Inheritance.** A London Story. Illustrated. Royal 16mo, 1*s.* 6*d.*

www.ingramcontent.com/pod-product-compliance
Lightning Source LLC
Chambersburg PA
CBHW022133160426
43197CB00009B/1270